The New Imperatives Educational Change

The New Imperatives of Educational Change is a clarion call to move beyond the standardized testing and marketplace competition that have become pervasive in school systems to focus instead on creating the conditions that will encourage all students to become critical and independent thinkers. Dennis Shirley presents five new imperatives to guide educators and policy makers toward a rethinking of what it means to teach effectively and to learn in depth. The *evidentiary* imperative requires educators to attain a better grasp of what data actually reveal about international trends in student learning. The *interpretive* imperative encourages mindful deliberation before acting on evidence in order to promote the integrity of a school community. The *professional* imperative describes new international research findings on promising pedagogies and curricula that propel learning in new directions. The *global* imperative argues that we all must look beyond our national boundaries to improve the flourishing of all young people, wherever they may be found. Finally, the *existential* imperative reminds us that students look to their teachers as role models who can dignify learning with meaning and embellish life with joy. Visionary in its scope and practical in its details, *The New Imperatives of Educational Change* is an indispensable road map for all teachers, principals, and system leaders.

Dennis Shirley is Professor of Education at the Lynch School of Education at Boston College and Editor-in-Chief of the *Journal of Educational Change*.

Routledge Leading Change Series
Edited by Andy Hargreaves and Pak Tee Ng

The New Imperatives of Educational Change

Achievement with Integrity

Dennis Shirley

Routledge
Taylor & Francis Group

NEW YORK AND LONDON

First published 2017
by Routledge
711 Third Avenue, New York, NY 10017

and by Routledge
2 Park Square, Milton Park, Abingdon, Oxon OX14 4RN

Routledge is an imprint of the Taylor & Francis Group, an informa business

Library of Congress Cataloging in Publication Data
Names: Shirley, Dennis, 1955- author.
Title: The new imperatives of educational change : achievement with integrity / by Dennis Shirley.
Description: New York : Routledge, 2016. | Series: Routledge leading change series | Includes bibliographical references and index.
Identifiers: LCCN 2016023512| ISBN 9781138926929 (hardback) | ISBN 9781138926936 (pbk.) | ISBN 9781315682907 (e-book)
Subjects: LCSH: Educational change. | Critical pedagogy. | Effective teaching. | Academic achievement.
Classification: LCC LB2806 .S46 2016 | DDC 370.1–dc23
LC record available at https://lccn.loc.gov/2016023512

ISBN: 978-1-138-92692-9 (hbk)
ISBN: 978-1-138-92693-6 (pbk)
ISBN: 978-1-315-68290-7 (ebk)

Typeset in Adobe Caslon
by Wearset Ltd, Boldon, Tyne and Wear

Printed in Canada

Dedicated to Laura Shelley Cochran
Educator Extraordinaire

Contents

Figures

Introduction

The Tipping Point for Educational Change

For decades, educational policy makers have been chipping away at school reform. Accountability and privatization have been their policy panaceas. It's been a demanding tour of duty, heavy on obligations and light on inspiration. In the US and elsewhere, the threat of pressure and the promise of support too often turned out to create excessive impositions unaccompanied by meaningful assistance. The result in many systems has been an exodus of educators toward fields that offer more creativity and innovation.

But at long last a more promising future for educational change is opening up before us. In the US the passage in 2015 of the Every Student Succeeds Act repudiated the intrusive prescriptiveness of the No Child Left Behind Act. Declining achievement results in other nations with similar policies have led leaders to reverse or at least rethink their assumptions. Student well-being, and not just student test scores, is given priority by parents, the public, and policy makers in many countries. Teacher unions are reinventing themselves, connecting their missions explicitly with student learning and with their own foundational aspirations for free and just societies. Digital technologies are giving students access to new worlds of knowledge that were previously beyond the reach of even the most specialized experts—and reformers are coming to realize that the impact on students' learning is greater when these technologies complement good teachers and teaching instead of replacing teachers completely.

We are poised on the verge of a global educational renaissance, unlike anything ever achieved in history. The Sustainable Development

Goals of the United Nations, endorsed by governments around the world, aspire to eliminate extreme poverty, provide universal primary and secondary education, expand access to health care, and to check and reverse climate change by 2030. Technological innovation, population mobility, climate change, and economic globalization are compelling all countries to recognize that their fates are inextricably intertwined with one another.

It is time for the world's educators to play a positive role in facing and overcoming the challenges that confront us. And many of them are more than ready.

But we only can meet these challenges if we free the education profession from the powerful distractors that have diverted and dissipated the precious energy of its members. None of these distractors has been greater than the simplistic and sometimes sinister misinterpretations of test score data that have driven massive and misdirected reform movements in education. Let's take just three examples.

- According to the Organization for Economic Cooperation and Development (OECD), the Chinese city of Shanghai has the world's most high-achieving system.[1] Shanghai receives first-rate rankings on literacy, math, and science on the Program of International Student Assessment (PISA) tests. But the public schools in relatively affluent Shanghai do not enroll students from other, more rural and impoverished parts of China. As is the case in Cuba, where students also score highly on international assessments, the Internet is censored in China. Dissidents are routinely arrested and incarcerated. *Should the school system in Shanghai be held up for emulation?*

- Right behind Shanghai, the Republic of South Korea receives top results on PISA, and its rankings have led many policy makers, including the US President, to laud its achievements. But South Korean students rank 65th out of 65—absolute rock bottom—according to an OECD survey measuring whether students feel good in school.[2] *Should educators sacrifice the happiness and mental health of young people in school in search of top test score results?*

- On two recent rankings of educational achievement, England was placed below average on one and in the top ten on the other.[3] It was average or below average on the different PISA subject areas of math, science, and literacy but it was a top performer in the Pearson Global Index of Cognitive Skills and Educational Attainment. How could this be? On Pearson's Global Index, England's results were aggregated with higher performers in the United Kingdom, such as Scotland and Northern Ireland. Pearson's indicators included elite powerhouses of higher education such as Oxford and Cambridge universities that have little to do with the quality of state schools at the primary and secondary level. *Are we paying sufficient attention to the manipulation of metrics that determine how nations are ranked?*

Increasingly, the public and the education profession understand that these questions are not merely rhetorical. Gone are the days when educational comparisons were restricted to cities, states, or provinces within nations. Education policy-making has gone global. It is a big business, with corporations focused on the profits they can make and the impacts they can achieve after detecting new opportunities for school improvement and innovations with new technologies around the world.

Some of this international connectivity is beneficial. Visitors to Finland have seen that teachers who use child-centered practices that allow for their professional judgment to be activated can produce higher results than their peers in other systems that are dominated by data-driven decision-making. Travelers to Singapore have seen how educators circulate among the Ministry of Education, the National Institute of Education, and the schools—consolidating a common mission and moving knowledge and expertise around as they do so. Educators who have visited Canada have seen how the Alberta Teachers' Association channels over 50 percent of its revenues into educators' professional development and research—and this has prompted these visitors to acknowledge the untapped educational leadership that exists in teacher unions. Germany and Switzerland are experiencing a surge of visitors who are interested in their traditions of vocational education and their contributions to economic innovation. Never before have educators and educational policy makers had so many opportunities to learn from one another on a global scale.

Too often, however, these opportunities have been squandered. Policies have been imported from other systems without paying attention to the deeper cultural understandings that have made them successful in the first place. For instance, while visitors to Finland learn that there are high standards for becoming a teacher, they then tear this one aspect of teacher quality out of context, and fail to acknowledge and address other equally influential forces that contribute to the success of the Finnish model. These include extensive public investment in early childhood education and an overall commitment to educational and social equity, including the empowerment of girls and women. Others grab the highly praised curriculum for Singapore math off the shelf but then teach it as technical problem solving. As a result, students do not gain the broader conceptual understanding that requires students to adjust their previous mental models about mathematics.

It's one thing to miss out on precious opportunities to improve students' learning because reform pressures in one's home country are too great and are insufficiently supported. But something far worse has occurred. When expectations keep escalating and sanctions are extreme, educators lose their moral compass. Today in the US hundreds of educators from Atlanta, El Paso, Philadelphia, Washington, DC, and other cities are either awaiting trial or are in prison for committing fraud by falsifying their students' test scores. These educators had made it their lives' work to serve students of color of low socio-economic status. Placing the onus of responsibility on them for their conduct is easy but simplistic. The educational policies that had been put in place, and those who supported them, are also implicated.[4]

In each of those cities, it is possible to point to indicators to argue that student test score results have been improving. In Atlanta, for example, results have moved up on a test called the "Trial Urban District Assessment" of the National Assessment of Educational Progress. African-American 4th graders' results at "basic" or above on reading have improved from 37 to 47 percent since 2003. In mathematics the proportion has increased from 50 to 72 percent.[5] Such results could be used to justify administrative policies that spread fear and intimidation throughout the district as schools with test score gains were celebrated and those that struggled were humiliated.

Significantly, no one to date has advanced such arguments. Why not? Everyone knows that what happened in Atlanta was wrong. No doubt about it: If you bully educators enough, you can get test score gains. But at some point you have to ask yourself what has become of your idealism. At such times it is essential to confront a painstakingly simple truth: *We have learned a great deal in recent years about how to raise student achievement scores, but we have not learned how to do this with integrity.*

"Integrity" comes from the Latin word "integritas" or "wholeness." When wholeness is attained, diverse parts of a system support one another. Educators' intrinsic motivation is ignited and students' natural enthusiasm for learning is awakened. Curricula are adapted to students' interests and needs, and assessment allows students to show not just what they don't know, but also what they do know. There is a dynamic cohesion in the system that drives everything forward toward a better future.

The central idea of this book is that we must indeed improve student achievement, and we must also ensure we do this with integrity. To do so we will need to ask fundamental questions. How can we inspire our young people not only with the temptations of a lucrative career, but also with aspirations to uplift others and to reach their full potential? How can we encourage them not only to be knowledge workers who will innovate with new technologies, but also to be social change agents who will exhibit the moral drive that animated Mahatma Gandhi, Rosa Parks, and Václav Havel? How can we make sure that our schools are inclusive of and inspiring for all kinds of students, including the eccentric individualists who are waiting to emerge as our next great poets, composers, and inventors?

It is time for educators and educational reformers to aspire to a broader vision of achievement and a deeper understanding of integrity. Achievement needs to encompass not just what is learned, or how that learning is scored, but also how to learn effectively. It needs to include not just tested subjects and skills such as reading, writing, and mathematics, but also those disciplines such as the arts, social studies, and the natural sciences that have been pushed to the margins. It is time to renew discussions about what makes for a good curriculum instead of just concentrating on how to prepare students for tests.

In recent years a narrow definition of academic achievement has been exposed as limited by a brilliant young class of digitally savvy entrepreneurs, many of whom did poorly in school because they had no outlets for their creativity. The rise of the new digital class has challenged educators to re-examine curricula and to explore new forms of blended learning that allow the young to bring their talents on their devices into the classroom. These are exciting developments, but we should be alert to problems technologies bring with them. If the implementation and spread of new technologies in schools is primarily driven by the profit motive and return on investment, the focus on learning gets lost. Digital personalization can also lead educators to neglect the socialization that requires face-to-face conversation and community building.

There is a lot more to achievement than personalized pathways and the prospects of corporate success. Achievement beyond academics should include the triumphs of immigrant youth who fled persecution at home to prevail with their cultural identity intact in a foreign land. It should include the sense of accomplishment of introverted youngsters who muster the courage to try out for the school play and discover that they have the stamina to overcome stage fright. In one small rural community with which I've been privileged to work, achievement beyond academics occurred when students rallied their community to support their principal who was battling brain cancer. These are experiences that cut through the verbiage and ideologies to get at what is most important in life: The aspiration to make a meaningful contribution, to conquer the fears that confront us, and to express our love and gratitude for others in their times of need.

From such experiences we learn that no one can be given integrity. It has to be earned. It won't be acquired by happenstance either. Integrity requires intentionality. We have to think as critically and creatively as we can, and come up with real, practical solutions.

How can we combine this broadened sense of achievement with integrity? This book proposes that integrity in our schools can be located in five new imperatives of educational change:

1 The courage to confront *evidence* of how students learn so as not to be blinded by simplistic ideologies.
2 The willingness to accept that in situations of ambiguity, educators must sensitively *interpret*, and not imperiously mandate, how to act on evidence.
3 The determination to study and learn from diverse *professional* solutions to pressing educational problems.
4 The aspiration to think in terms of the *global* ramifications of educational policies and practices.
5 The adaptability to acknowledge that the *existential* realities of students' lives matter and that schools can and should help students to make meaning of their experiences.

To achieve integrity in a new millennium, we will have to evolve beyond an exclusive focus on big data to an inclusive culture of big ideas. We must inspire our students with the excitement of intellectual discovery, the pursuit of physical health, the majesty of nature, and the powerful and sustaining bonds of community.

The coming chapters show that the reigning imperatives that some nations have prescribed for educators for years have become stale and stagnant. Fresh winds are blowing in from all directions. From Singapore to Sweden and from California to Chile, a global paradigm shift is underway. We are at a tipping point for educational change.

Notes

1 OECD (2013) *PISA 2012 results in focus: What 15-year-olds know and what they do with what they know.* Paris: OECD.
2 OECD, *PISA 2012 results in focus*, p. 21.
3 Smithers, A. (2013) *Confusion in the ranks: How good are England's schools?* Buckingham, England: Centre for Education and Employment Research, University of Buckingham.
4 Quinton, S. (2015, May 8) In wake of cheating disgrace, are Atlanta schools improving? *The Atlantic.* Retrieved from www.theatlantic.com/politics/archive/2015/05/in-wake-of-cheating-disgrace-are-atlanta-schools-improving/432012/. Fernandez, M. (2012, October 13) El Paso schools confront scandal of students who "disappeared" at

test time. *New York Times*. Retrieved from www.nytimes.com/2012/10/14/education/
el-paso-rattled-by-scandal-of-disappeared-students.html?_r=0. Rich, M., & Hurdle, J.
(2014, January 13) Erased answers on tests in Philadelphia lead to a three-year cheating scandal. *New York Times*. Retrieved from www.nytimes.com/2014/01/24/us/
erased-answers-on-tests-in-philadelphia-lead-to-a-three-year-cheating-scandal.html.
Kerchner, C.T. (2013, April 21) DC cheating issue calls test-driven incentives into
question. EdSource. Retrieved from http://edsource.org/2013/d-c-cheating-issue-
calls-test-driven-incentives-into-question/30754.
5 Quinton, In wake of cheating disgrace, p. 3.

References

Fernandez, M. (2012, October 13) El Paso schools confront scandal of students who "disappeared" at test time. *New York Times*. Retrieved from
www.nytimes.com/2012/10/14/education/el-paso-rattled-by-scandal-of-
disappeared-students.html?_r=0.

Kerchner, C.T. (2013, April 21) DC cheating issue calls test-driven incentives
into question. EdSource. Retrieved from http://edsource.org/2013/d-c-
cheating-issue-calls-test-driven-incentives-into-question/30754.

OECD (2013) *PISA 2012 results in focus: What 15-year-olds know and what
they do with what they know.* Paris: OECD.

Quinton, S. (2015, May 8) In wake of cheating disgrace, are Atlanta schools
improving? *The Atlantic*. Retrieved from www.theatlantic.com/politics/
archive/2015/05/in-wake-of-cheating-disgrace-are-atlanta-schools-
improving/432012/.

Rich, M., & Hurdle, J. (2014, January 13) Erased answers on tests in Philadelphia lead to a three-year cheating scandal. *New York Times*.
Retrieved from www.nytimes.com/2014/01/24/us/erased-answers-on-
tests-in-philadelphia-lead-to-a-three-year-cheating-scandal.html.

Smithers, A. (2013) *Confusion in the ranks: How good are England's schools?*
Buckingham, England: Centre for Education and Employment
Research, University of Buckingham.

1

IMPERATIVES OLD AND NEW

In an ideal world, students and teachers would thrive in classes full of purposeful learning. But in schools as they are today, too many educators report the opposite. In studies I have conducted in North America, they have frequently complained about high levels of constraint upon their professional judgment. One principal in a policy environment that emphasizes competition describes how "much of what we do every day is to market ourselves. We need to keep parents happy so we have good accountability results. I have become, in many ways, more of a marketing manager than an educator." Another principal in a district that now requires that she spend much of her time evaluating teachers complains about how "It's pulled me in a lot of different directions." In addition to all the time taken up with evaluations, she says,

> You have parental involvement activities that you're trying to plan for. You're meeting with different groups to try to get new instructional practices in place. It makes it difficult to do all of the things you're trying to do. It becomes an impossible job.

These concerns reflect the long-term trend over previous decades toward higher levels of pressure on educators, increased accountability, and greater uniformity. Ironically, it was market competitiveness that promised innovation that often provoked this standardization, because schools can't be ranked with one another without a common set of measures. Likewise, educators' efficacy can't be compared on systems of teacher quality without shared evaluation protocols and tests. The more competitive education has become, the more that uniform assessments have been needed to measure performance.

As if this push for compliance and conformity was not enough, educators have also found themselves faced with contradictory expectations to turn out students who are critical thinkers and creative problem solvers. But an excess of metrics has marginalized creativity in teaching and therefore also in learning. These constraining imperatives act as commands for professional compliance. They impose on teachers questionable pedagogies and curriculum materials that are unsuited to the learning demands of today's complex societies.

These old imperatives of educational change are the result of policies that have been in place for over a quarter of a century and that have been codified into law, then mandated upon schools. They are:

1   An *ideological imperative* that has emphasized market competition, testing, and standardization as levers to improve schools—despite the absence of evidence to support these directions.

2   An *imperial imperative* that has projected this ideology onto other schools and systems as the best way to move forward, even when those other systems were already succeeding by employing different ways to organize their work.

3   A *prescriptive imperative* that has mandated the daily work of educators from higher levels of school bureaucracies.

4   An *insular imperative* that overloaded educators with so many policy demands that their ability to learn from other schools and systems elsewhere has been seriously impeded.

5   An *instrumental imperative* that has defined students and teachers in relation to their economic contributions, with a concomitant disregard for values of compassion, solidarity, or service.

These five old imperatives of educational change directed educators toward attaining one common objective: testing for fidelity. Pedagogy, curriculum, and assessments became tightly aligned with one another. Electives, project-based learning, and interdisciplinary programs of study were replaced with mandated curriculum carefully geared to the tests. Teacher education programs and teacher salary schedules were transformed. The old imperatives aggressively marketed frontal instruction, standardized curricula, and pervasive test-based competition.

As official government policies, the old imperatives spread like wildfire. They are contrasted with the five new imperatives in Figure 1.1.

In the countries most infatuated with the old imperatives, student achievement results have remained at lackluster levels or have declined precipitously. Parents, students, and professionals have become increasingly alienated. One out of every five students in New York State declined to take the state's standardized examinations. Students and teachers in Chile led massive street protests against their country's privatized system. Professional associations around the world communicated that their members were fed up. The critics were supported by the OECD's findings that "school choice—and by extension, school competition—is related to greater levels of

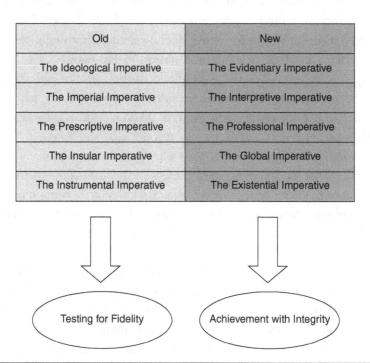

Old	New
The Ideological Imperative	The Evidentiary Imperative
The Imperial Imperative	The Interpretive Imperative
The Prescriptive Imperative	The Professional Imperative
The Insular Imperative	The Global Imperative
The Instrumental Imperative	The Existential Imperative

Testing for Fidelity   Achievement with Integrity

Figure 1.1 Old and New Imperatives of Educational Change.

segregation in the school system."[1] True believers in the old imperatives advocated pushing on harder, but in many ways they overplayed
their hand. This book will show that a new agenda with an accompanying set of new imperatives is now emerging instead.

Chapter 2 examines data from three countries—England, the US,
and Sweden—that institutionalized the old imperatives to the great-
est degree. It argues that it is time to replace an old *ideological imperative* that has undergirded policies for years with a new, *evidentiary
imperative*. To do so it is necessary to explore the rise and spread of
an ideology of educational change that prioritized markets, testing,
and standardization. This ideology promised innovation and
improved learning results, but the opposite occurred. Results either
stalled or declined, in some cases precipitously.

The *ideological imperative* has been pursued not only in the absence
of supportive evidence but also through selective and manipulative
use of the evidence that exists. For instance, in an impactful report
by McKinsey & Company on successful educational systems, high-
achieving Finland was completely omitted.[2] With its emphases on
equity, inclusion, and social democracy, the Finnish model contra-
dicted McKinsey's push for markets, choice, and accountability.

Germany is often held up as a nation to emulate because of its
rising results on PISA. In a dramatic display of the old *imperial
imperative*, Germany's improving results have been erroneously credited by US experts to the same policies that have actually contributed
to the troubling outcomes for England, the US, and Sweden.[3] These
have forced the German data into a market fundamentalist framework. In Chapter 3, a critique of these misattributions opens the way
for a more nuanced *interpretative imperative* that goes beyond imposing ideology onto other nations. Instead, the *interpretive imperative*
seeks to understand Germany and other systems on their own terms,
from the inside out.

On one occasion, I asked a Finnish educator what American educators would have to do to attain Finland's high PISA results using
similar strategies. "It's easy," he said, "All you have to do is to share
our history!" But who would sacrifice their own culture, in order to
improve their country's PISA results? Since cultures and histories
vary around the globe, we can no more teleport strategies from one

place to another than we can give up cultural practices that are as pervasive as the air we breathe. We can study data and develop interpretations, to be sure. But direct imitation rarely works—if ever.

This does not mean, however, that there is no hope for educators. The third new imperative of educational change, and the subject of Chapter 4, is *the professional imperative*. In what does this consist, and why does it matter?

For decades educators have struggled to evolve beyond the status of what Amitai Etzioni described as a "semi-profession."[4] For Etzioni, teachers could not be defined as true professionals because they lacked administrative control of their work, relied primarily on outsiders for increasing their knowledge base, and were unable to close ranks to create a unified guild. Educators were not like lawyers, doctors, or engineers. They were like social workers and nurses.

Etzioni was a sociologist. He was not troubled by a lack of professionalism in education. In fact, he argued that once educators learned to accept the lowly status of their work, "the dysfunctional consequences of attempts to pass will tend to disappear. The semi-professions will be able to be themselves."[5]

From today's vantage point, Etzioni's injunction for educators to acquiesce to semi-professional status was disastrous. The economy of today increasingly rewards knowledge workers who are able to work with large amounts of abstract information rapidly, efficiently, and with versatility.[6] Such skills are not innate. They have to be taught to students over many years through carefully scaffolded pedagogy with outstanding curricula. These skills will not be acquired from those who are not flexible knowledge workers themselves. Students will only learn the skills and dispositions of knowledge workers from teachers who themselves are knowledge workers.

In 2003 Andy Hargreaves argued that the "key reform imperatives" of that time were "preparing people neither for the knowledge economy nor for public life beyond it."[7] For Hargreaves, it wasn't enough to prepare students to be knowledge workers, because this could blind them to the inhumane and socially unjust conditions of market economies. Instead, students needed to learn beyond the knowledge economy, so that they would have the humanistic social skills to restore community, enhance cosmopolitanism, and preserve an endangered ecosystem.

More than a decade was lost ignoring this clarion call for change. In the interim, a *prescriptive imperative* reigned. Under this imperative, educators' judgment was diminished and the hierarchical and administrative control of educators was intensified. This was the opposite of a professionalizing agenda. So we have to make up for lost time. How we move from prescription to professionalism is the third new imperative of educational change.

The good news is that there is an increasing consensus of what this entails. In 2012 Hargreaves and co-author Michael Fullan published a new conceptual framework for educators entitled *Professional Capital*.[8] This disaggregated educators' professionalism into three components:

1   the *human capital*, or economic value, of what individuals know;
2   the *social capital*, or relational trust, that builds collaborative capacity amongst colleagues; and
3   the *decisional capital*, or the ability of individuals to make good judgments when faced with incomplete or conflicting evidence.

Shortly after *Professional Capital* appeared, the OECD published updated findings from its 2009 and 2012 Teaching and Learning International Survey (TALIS), the world's largest surveys of teachers.[9] Andreas Schleicher, the OECD Director of the Directorate for Education and Skills, then developed a TALIS index of teacher professionalism, with the following three components:

1   the "knowledge-based best practices" of the individual;
2   peer networks;
3   autonomy, with reference to decision-making over such matters as curriculum, assessment, and student discipline.[10]

It is striking how much the professional capital framework and the TALIS frameworks harmonize with one another. Human capital is similar to knowledge-based practices. Social capital relates to peer networks. Decisional capital parallels autonomy. The professional capital and TALIS frameworks combined provide a unified approach to uplift the status of the teaching profession. This is a historical paradigm shift away from micromanagement and control to moral judgment and continual learning, for educators as well as for their students.

These developments provide the point of departure for a new *professional imperative* that is intended to augment both the professional capital and TALIS frameworks. Chapter 4 provides illustrations of the *professional imperative* at work in diverse jurisdictions that are reinventing what it means to learn, to teach, and to collaborate. From Singapore to Mexico to the US educators are busily working out new practices and theories of teaching and learning that point us toward a better future for all.

Unfortunately and ironically, the way in which many international assessments are interpreted by policy organizations and public media exacerbates educational nationalism and exceptionalism. Anything but a top ranking result can be used by political opponents to score points in debates. But shouldn't we all be pleased if any educational system is improving? Surely it is better for all of us if the collective knowledge of humanity is enhanced, even amongst nations that, in some ways, are economic competitors. If we are to overcome the trap of zero-sum reasoning, then this old *insular imperative* must give way to a *global imperative* of educational change. This will value human lives equally wherever the young may be found.

What does and should this *global imperative* look like? One view is that of Kishore Mahbubani, Dean of the Lee Kwan Yew School of Public Policy at the National University of Singapore. He describes the current era as a time of "great convergence" when technology and trade are throwing all of the world's peoples into increasingly productive interaction with one another.[11] Many experience the great convergence as an unmitigated blessing as competition drives down prices, traditional hierarchies are overthrown, and new opportunities open up for cross-cultural learning and exchange. Educators in all parts of the world now are encountering students from diverse cultures in their classrooms, with a wealth of new opportunities for developing greater global awareness amongst all of their students.[12] New technologies are facilitating much of this exchange as a phone call to a neighbor now costs as much as a Skype call to the other side of the world.

Not all observers are as optimistic as Mahbubani, though.[13] Their fear is that convergence undermines the positive aspects of their local and national cultures, not through the new learning communities that are created in schools, but rather because of larger market-driven forces that erode traditional values and replace them with materialism.

Our challenge in relation to global convergence is to make the most of its blessings while overcoming its problematic aspects. Kwame Anthony Appiah provides tools and principles with which to do this in *Cosmopolitanism: Ethics in a World of Strangers*.[14] We must accept one another's differences, Appiah says, but this does not mean that we are recused from dialogue. Differences must not stop conversations; they must initiate them. Only then can we realize our potential for improving the human condition.

Education has a key role to play in optimizing convergence in a thoughtful and critical way. We need to ask educators and those they educate to analyze and address the epochal challenges of our time. These include eliminating poverty, promoting health and education around the world, and securing environmental sustainability. Now is the time to marshal the same kind of collective willpower that has slain so many lions of injustice in the past. Human beings do not have to live out lives of grinding poverty. Warfare is not inevitable. Illiteracy does not have to persist forever. Girls everywhere have the same right to attend school as boys. We have the power to rally our collective conscience and to build a better future that is uplifting for all.

As we do so, however, we will need to attend to another dimension of change that has been neglected for years and now is receiving increasing attention from policy makers around the world. Throughout much of the reform literature in recent years has run the theme of students as future wage earners. While we should want education to confer economic value on our students, care must be taken that we do not limit our understandings of education to students' potential salaries. To do so is to fall prey to an *instrumental imperative* that views students' education only as means to something else, and not as its own end.

We know a great deal about how students judge their life satisfaction through student surveys.[15] But why is it that rates of depression and anxiety have been soaring among young people in the economically developed world?[16] Why is a heroin epidemic now damaging learning in many schools, including those in affluent communities?[17]

At least part of the answer resides in the mechanical way that education has been conceived in terms of inputs and outputs. This has implicitly and persistently undermined other aspects of the human condition, such as the quest for meaning and belonging. The rhetoric of data-driven decision-making, so prominent in recent years, has crowded out the instructional space needed for reflections on what it means to be fully alive and what it means to be thrown into relationships of mutual dependency. Unlike upper secondary schools in Europe that offer philosophy for adolescents, schools in North America do not even include this subject in the curriculum. The visual and performing arts, which provide students for venues to express what is inside of them, have always been the first curricular areas to be cut.

For some, new technologies provide venues for the "personalization" of education that can provide meaning to the young. New technologies allow friendships to be forged across international lines and have unleashed a wealth of talent from unexpected sources. They do not, however, have an inherent capacity to address the needs of the young for a sense of purpose and belonging. While the Internet can serve to connect individuals from around the world through gaming, for example, in other cases gaming increases social isolation when the young want to go beyond superficial transactions into areas involving trust and vulnerability.[18]

The fifth, *existential imperative* requires us to provide our students with opportunities to explore the human quest for meaning. Meaning is different from well-being, which increasingly is being defined in ways that could lead to political passivity and self-absorption among the young.[19] The struggle for meaning necessarily requires difficulty and discomfort as one engages with the scope of human suffering and the catastrophe of environmental degradation. This will not always make for the trendy, happy-go-lucky attitudes that we might wish for the young, but it will make them more thoughtful and potentially compassionate global citizens.

Is this legitimate terrain for educators? The world's great religions and philosophies, whether of Occident or Orient, of the global South or North, have always been concerned with the formation of the subjective sides of life. This is why the world's cultures have given so much attention to the arts, poetry, literature, and philosophy.

How this quest for meaning will occur should not be prescribed. You can't mandate meaning! You can, however, provide students with opportunities to explore how they can give meaning to their lives. This requires a different set of skills and dispositions for educators than the press for results. It requires time and space not only for information to be learned, but also for ideas to germinate. It requires that educators recover some of the lost pastoral and moral dimensions of their craft that have been eroded in an age of instrumental rationality. It will not come of its own accord. It will require a fundamental recalibration of how we relate achievement and integrity.

Intentions and Results

In education, recent reforms have emphasized that results matter most. This is called utilitarianism in philosophy.[20] In the crudest forms of utilitarianism, it doesn't matter how you reach your objectives. For educators, simplistic utilitarianism has led to policies focused on test scores. This has often crowded out other important educational purposes. In the worst manifestations of the old imperatives, educators force students to march through the curriculum, testing them for fidelity each step of the way.

The alternative to utilitarianism in moral philosophy is intentionalism.[21] Intentionalists observe that you can't control everything or even most things in life, but you can control your intentions. Intentionalists are more concerned than utilitarians with why a goal is worthy in the first place. They are more alert to the ways in which a rigid fixation on a goal at one point in time could impede necessary reflection at a point further along in the future when contexts may have changed, or when young people aren't responding to the goal of testing with fidelity. Intentionalists want achievement, but not at the cost of their integrity.

In educational change utilitarians focus on student achievement, and intentionalists insist on professional integrity. The utilitarians have dominated change agendas for years but increasingly the profession, students, and parents want a more balanced approach that harmonizes achievement with integrity. But what would this look like? The quadrant depicted in Figure 1.2 below provides a visual representation, accompanied by illustrations of the ways in which achievement has interacted with integrity in schools in recent years.

Low Achievement, Low Integrity

The sure way to hit the Ground Zero of educational change is to organize school systems so that individuals have neither achievement nor integrity. I've worked with many teacher leadership initiatives in the US and abroad and have had many opportunities to learn about the impact of policies on students and teachers. While the intentions behind the No Child Left Behind Act in the US and similar policies in other countries were laudable, in practice the demands for rapidly rising test scores resulted in neither improved achievement nor increased integrity.   *ECLB*

Figure 1.2 Quadrant Depicting Four Dimensions of Achievement with Integrity.

In "Mindful Teacher Seminars" I have led with teacher leader Elizabeth MacDonald, teachers described working in schools in which a carousel of principals came and went with precious little time to build team spirit and raise morale before they were fired, sometimes in only one year, as a result of stalled test scores.[22] Teachers were "clipboarded" by anonymous evaluators who appeared at random, filled out check-lists, and disappeared, with no opportunities for feedback and discussion. Schools eradicated free play, except for Fridays, with the sanction of denying recess if students misbehaved. Music and art were slashed back even as early as kindergarten so that teachers had more time to prepare students for the tests that they would take at grade 3. Test preparatory activities filled the curriculum, and students were warned that if their test results weren't good, their school could be closed. "Morning meetings," instead of being a time for students to discuss how they were learning together, were given over to school-wide meetings in which anxious principals made students listen to lengthy exhortations to follow rules, respect their teachers, and improve their test scores.

Occasionally such schools could boost results for a year or two, especially if they benefited from talented coaches provided by a partnering university or were fortunate to hire intrepid veterans who knew ways to inspire staff and motivate students. On the whole, however, schools suffered from churning leadership, staff, and programs. Teachers understood the logic of pacing guides but found that when they were supervised too rigidly they lacked enough time to adapt materials for struggling students. Teachers resented the amount of time given over to pre-tests and post-tests that provided data for central office staff but could have been better used for instruction. The special circumstances of immigrant, transnational, or indigenous students did not fit with standardized, prescribed instruction, but teachers were expected to persist even when the prescribed strategies weren't working.

For their part, principals were caught in the middle. They were told by inspirational speakers to create professional learning communities but in practice were pushed by central office to render them as "data teams." Educators who persisted with field trips to museums or to the aquarium fell out of favor.

Schooling has to be more than an endless grind. It has to use every resource available to motivate students and staff. Small wonder, then, that when principals adopted leadership techniques of command and control they were unable to lift up student achievement. They also failed to manifest professional integrity.

High Achievement, Low Integrity

Authoritarian governments are often praised for their educational systems by international commentators who ignore the limitations of their citizens' freedom of speech. This blindness to the suppression of not only student voice, but that of their educators as well, represents a failure to uphold human rights. "There was much wrong with the German Democratic Republic (GDR), but their education system was not one of them," states the widely cited *Strong Performers and Successful Reformers in Education.*[23] Likewise, in *Cuba's Academic Advantage: Why Students in Cuba Do Better in School*, Martin Carnoy barely touches upon the censorship that has been a hallmark of that island's communist regime.[24] The adulation heaped upon the schools of Shanghai after their PISA results were posted in 2012 reveals a readiness not only to accommodate, but also to celebrate schools in which young people and their educators have no opportunities to question their governments.[25]

We shouldn't be surprised that young people in a number of authoritarian systems do well on international assessments such as PISA. Imagine how much easier it would be to teach students if they never raised impertinent questions, and if you could rely on your government to imprison them if they persisted! Education in such systems can work as a highly synchronized machine, but it by definition cannot produce individuals who like to innovate, take pleasure in nonconformity, and throw groupthink into disarray by introducing hitherto unimagined possibilities into the midst of conversations. Such systems will always be dependent on others to come up with new inventions. They can indeed mass produce others' commodities at a profit as long as employee wages remain low by international standards and the workforce is unorganized. There is little inspiring here when one looks up close at what really is transpiring. There is high achievement in name only, with integrity a topic only to be mentioned in an unread addendum in the bottom of the drawer.

High Integrity, Low Achievement

Ideally, high integrity would always lead to high achievement. Unfortunately, educational change isn't so simple. I recently led a Boston College team to review the leadership strategy in the public school system in a southern city in the US. As part of this review we interviewed school principals, teachers, and central office staff in the system. This gave us a good overview of the diversity of school leadership in the city. One school demonstrated the conundrum of high integrity combined with low achievement.

This elementary school was in one of the poorest parts of the city and had some of the lowest achievement results in the state. Desperate for positive traction, the district placed a popular minister of a community church who was also a teacher as a new principal in the school. The principal brought evangelical fervor to his role. "I love doing this because I love humankind," he said. "I think you have to love humankind. Parents have to feel confident that we are here first to love, but love means making you do right, you know. I will make you do right because I love you."

The new principal thrived on being at the center of activity. "I love to be maxed out," he said. "I'm going to die on my feet." He was constantly observing instruction. "I spend probably 75 to 80 percent of my day in and out of classrooms," he stated, asking "How am I going to know what you're doing in your classroom if I'm not there?" For him, parental involvement was key: "I'm out in the building shaking hands, talking eyeball to eyeball, going down to the community. I don't care if they have a beer bottle in their hands. It ain't about that. I'm there for the kids."

In high-poverty communities, principals with affirmative messages are indispensable. In terms of his dedication to the school and its community, this principal was an undeniable asset. But interviews with teachers revealed a problematic side to his leadership. Consultants had introduced instructional walkthroughs to the school, but teachers who had observed their colleagues "were told not to talk with them," one teacher said. "We weren't supposed to talk about, you know, exactly what the teachers were doing." Evaluations were the exclusive domain of the principal. As a consequence, teachers' capacities to form good judgments about teaching were not developed. The teachers recognized this. One said, "We still have a long way to go."

This principal exhibited personal integrity. He worked tirelessly for his school. But in spite of his high moral values, his leadership style did not improve achievement. He gave no evidence of providing specific feedback on particular strategies to his staff. His comments floated in the realm of generalities rather than specific recommendations for action. While his work with his congregation had positive aspects in terms of community relations, it also was a distraction. When I visited his school for interviews and focus group discussions, he fielded calls from his church of over 400 members throughout the day.

Three years later results had not improved in the school. It remained mired in the bottom 1 percent on state assessments. Under pressure from district leaders, the principal retired. Having failed to develop local expertise, the district hired a turnaround expert from out of state. Integrity in terms of intentions had not led to achievement in results.

High Achievement, High Integrity

The fourth and final category connects high achievement with high integrity. We can find many examples of this in schools today. Orchard Gardens K-8 School in Boston underwent a renaissance when Principal Andrew Bott fired the schools' security guards and used the funding to hire arts teachers instead. Teachers were given time to collaborate and the school day was extended and enriched with cultural activities. Orchard Gardens had experienced five principals in the previous seven years and over 50 percent of the staff had left at the end of each school year.

Bott changed this pervasive sense of crisis with an insistently positive message of belief in students' potential. He began "shout-outs" over the school intercom that celebrated students' achievements. He empowered art faculty to redesign the interior of the building with brightly colored student art that showed off their burgeoning talents. Students with negative attitudes were given musical instruments and instruction to help them to channel their energies in a positive direction. With a reinvented culture Orchard Gardens became one of the most rapidly improving schools in Massachusetts, with English language, arts, and mathematics results increasing by 50 percent or more on the state's Massachusetts Comprehensive Assessment System (MCAS) tests.[26]

Another example of high achievement with high integrity comes from Germany. The Robert Bosch Comprehensive School in the small northern city of Hildesheim was established to create a more democratic school environment than traditional tracked secondary schools allowed. When given the choice, however, students gravitated toward either the elite *Gymnasium* or more vocationally oriented schools. Years before "instructional rounds" became popular, the Bosch School's faculty responded to their enrollment deficit by creating their own protocol for visiting each other's classes and improving their teaching. As is common in Germany, headmaster Wilfried Kretschmer taught his own classes in the school. His colleagues assessed his teaching just as he assessed theirs.

In Germany, schools' achievement results are not published by the government, which prefers to use results for diagnostic rather than competitive purposes. In one year, however, the results were leaked to the press. They revealed that the Bosch School's results exceeded those of the neighboring elite *Gymnasia*. The school's homegrown model of teachers helping one another to get better received national attention and sparked a new reform movement of collaborative professionalism that now places Germany ahead of other countries.[27]

Orchard Gardens and the Bosch School exemplify achievement with integrity. In each case the preferred leadership strategy was that of creating teams of professionals that study evidence, interpret it collaboratively, and develop new pedagogical approaches that spread throughout a school or a network. Educators activate themselves to take charge of teaching and learning and do so in a climate of shared moral purpose. There are no miracles here, and while allies from higher education are valued, the real action happens in the school on a daily basis. As a consequence, students achieve at increasingly higher levels, guided forward by teams of educators who insist on the integrity of an uncompromising professional ethos.

A New Paradigm

Achievement and integrity should not be opposites but complementary components of a balanced education. Excessive attention to achievement robs students of the pleasures of learning and sacrifices the present for the future. Too much devotion to the ideal of integrity yields high moral principles but may lead to neglect of the skills needed to raise achievement. Left on its own, each approach is one-sided.

We need a new paradigm. This should combine achievement with integrity. This must be done in ways that are internally consistent and make sense on a practical level for educators and for students.

What does this mean for the old and new imperatives of educational change?

When achievement and integrity are harmonized, improvement efforts are based on intelligent interpretations of evidence, including the evidence of what really makes other schools and systems successful. This is the *evidentiary imperative*. When you have achievement with integrity, you learn from others' success but do not impose the preferred model of one country on educational systems elsewhere. This is the *interpretive imperative*.

Achievement with integrity also involves teachers being able and allowed to exercise professional judgments in their classrooms, not in an arbitrary or capricious way, but based on the expertise they develop autonomously through independent study, and in collaboration with their colleagues in peer networks. This is the *professional imperative*. Fourth, achievement with integrity means engaging with the wider world beyond one's own borders as a classroom teacher and as a constantly learning professional. This is the *global imperative*. Finally, achievement with integrity means that we pay attention to the quest for meaning within a wider community, rather than only acquiring the skills to be economically productive. This is the *existential imperative*.

Can we address each and all of these new imperatives—evidentiary, interpretive, professional, global, and existential—in order to attain achievement with integrity? We all feel disheartened from time to time—none more than those dedicated educators who commit themselves to the most challenging schools and the most poorly resourced communities for decades. But we don't have to resort to gaming the system or polishing our school branding strategies to climb up the tested achievement rankings. We can instead become inveterate scouts of promising, evidence-informed strategies—from the classroom next door to the other side of the world. We can also rededicate ourselves to the promise of learning as a form of human fulfillment for the sake of a better future.

These imperatives are based on evidence but not beaten down by it. They uplift professional judgment without placing it on a pedestal. And they ask of teachers no more than most teachers have ever asked of themselves—to work hard and work together to exercise their duty of care for all their students and their responsibility to educate every one of them to the best of their ability.

Notes

1 OECD (2012) *PISA 2012 results: What makes schools successful? Resources, policies and practices, volume 4*. Paris: OECD, p. 54.
2 Mourshed, M., Chijioke, C., & Barber, M. (2010) *How the worlds' most improved school systems keep getting better*. London: McKinsey & Company.
3 OECD (2010) *Strong performers and successful reformers: Lessons from PISA for the United States*. Paris: OECD.
4 Etzioni, A. (1969) *The semi-professions and their organization: Teachers, nurses, social workers*. New York: Free Press, p. viii.
5 Etzioni, *The semi-professions*, p. vii.
6 Cortada, J.W. (1998). *The rise of the knowledge worker*. Woburn, MA: Butterworth-Heinemann.
7 Hargreaves, A. (2003) *Teaching in the knowledge society: Education in the age of insecurity*. New York: Teachers College Press, p. 5.
8 Hargreaves, A., & Fullan, M. (2012) *Professional capital: Transforming teaching in every school*. New York: Teachers College Press.
9 OECD (2014) *TALIS 2013 results: An international perspective on teaching and learning*. Paris: OECD.
10 Schleicher, A. (2016) *Teaching excellence through professional learning and policy reform: Lessons from around the world*. Paris: OECD, p. 37.
11 Mahbubani, K. (2013) *The great convergence: Asia, the west, and the logic of one world*. New York: Public Affairs, p. 1.
12 Skerrett, A. (2015) *Teaching transnational youth: Literacy and education in a changing world*. New York: Teachers College Press.

13 See Chen, K.-H. (2010) *Asia as method: Toward deimperialization*. Durham, NC: Duke University Press, and Mishra, P. (2012) *From the ruins of empire: The revolt against the west and the making of Asia*. London: Penguin.

14 Appiah, K.A. (2006) *Cosmopolitanism: Ethics in a world of strangers*. New York: Norton.

15 UNICEF (2013) *Child well-being in rich countries: A comparative overview*. Florence: Innocenti.

16 Luthar, S.S., Barkin, S.H., & Crossman, E.J. (2013) "I can, therefore I must": Fragility in the upper-middle classes. *Developmental Psychopathology* 25(2), 1529–1549.

17 Centers for Disease Control and Prevention (2015) *Today's heroin epidemic*. Retrieved from www.cdc.gov/vitalsigns/heroin/.

18 Aboujjaoude, E. (2011) *Virtually you: The dangerous powers of the e-personality*. New York: Norton. Carr, N. (2010) *The shallows: What the internet is doing to our brains*. New York: Norton.

19 Burkeman, O. (2012) *The antidote: Happiness for people who can't stand positive thinking*. New York: Faber & Faber.

20 Mill, J.S. (1861/1985) *Utilitarianism*. New York: Macmillan.

21 Kant, I. (1785/2002) *Groundwork for the metaphysics of morals*. New Haven: Yale University Press.

22 Shirley, D., & MacDonald, E. (2016) *The mindful teacher*. New York: Teachers College Press.

23 OECD, *Strong performers and successful reformers*, p. 207.

24 Carnoy, M. (2007) *Cuba's academic advantage: Why students in Cuba do better in school*. Stanford: Stanford University Press.

25 See for example Tan, C. (2013) *Learning from Shanghai: Lessons on achieving educational success*. Dordrecht, Holland: Springer, and Tucker, M.S. (Ed.) (2011) *Surpassing Shanghai: An agenda for American education built on the world's leading systems*. Cambridge, MA: Harvard Education Press. For a critical perspective see Zhao, Y. (2014) *Who's afraid of the big bad dragon? Why China has the best (and worst) education system in the world*. San Francisco: Jossey-Bass.

26 McGuinness, W. (2013, May 10) Orchard Gardens principal Andrew Bott fires security, hires art teachers, revitalizes school. *Huffington Post*. Retrieved from www. huffingtonpost.com/2013/05/02/orchard-gardens-andrew-bott_n_3202426.html.

27 The transformation of the Robert Bosch Comprehensive School is described in detail the untranslated doctoral dissertation of its principal: Kretschmer, W. (2014) *Demokratische Leistungsschule: Pädagogische Kultur in Unternehmerischen Formen* [Democratic achievement school: Pedagogical culture in innovative forms]. Friedrich-Schiller-University, Jena. On the impact of the school's improvement model, see Otto, J., & Spiewak, M. (2016, February 25) Nie mehr allein [Never again alone]. *Die Zeit*, p. 65. On higher levels of teacher cooperation in Germany than in the other countries of the OECD, see Richter, D., & Pant, H.A. (2016) *Lehrerkooperation in Deutschland* [Teacher cooperation in Germany]. Gütersloh, Germany: Bertelsmann Foundation.

References

Aboujjaoude, E. (2011) *Virtually you: The dangerous powers of the e-personality*. New York: Norton.

Appiah, K.A. (2006) *Cosmopolitanism: Ethics in a world of strangers*. New York: Norton.

Burkeman, O. (2012) *The antidote: Happiness for people who can't stand positive thinking*. New York: Faber & Faber.

Carnoy, M. (2007) *Cuba's academic advantage: Why students in Cuba do better in school*. Stanford: Stanford University Press.

Carr, N. (2010) *The shallows: What the internet is doing to our brains*. New York: Norton.

Centers for Disease Control and Prevention (2015) *Today's heroin epidemic*. Retrieved from www.cdc.gov/vitalsigns/heroin/.

Chen, K.-H. (2010) *Asia as method: Toward deimperialization*. Durham, NC: Duke University Press.

Cortada, J.W. (1998). *The rise of the knowledge worker*. Woburn, MA: Butterworth-Heinemann.

Etzioni, A. (1969) *The semi-professions and their organization: Teachers, nurses, social workers*. New York: Free Press.

Hargreaves, A. (2003) *Teaching in the knowledge society: Education in the age of insecurity*. New York: Teachers College Press.

Hargreaves, A., & Fullan, M. (2012) *Professional capital: Transforming teaching in every school*. New York: Teachers College Press.

Kant, I. (1785/2002) *Groundwork for the metaphysics of morals*. New Haven: Yale University Press.

Kretschmer, W. (2014) *Demokratische Leistungsschule: Pädagogische Kultur in Unternehmerischen Formen* [Democratic achievement school: Pedagogical culture in innovative forms]. Friedrich-Schiller-University, Jena.

Luthar, S.S., Barkin, S.H., & Crossman, E.J. (2013) "I can, therefore I must": Fragility in the upper-middle classes. *Developmental Psychopathology* 25(2), 1529–1549.

McGuinness, W. (2013, May 10) Orchard Gardens principal Andrew Bott fires security, hires art teachers, revitalizes school. *Huffington Post*. Retrieved from www.huffingtonpost.com/2013/05/02/orchard-gardens-andrew-bott_n_3202426.html.

Mahbubani, K. (2013) *The great convergence: Asia, the west, and the logic of one world*. New York: Public Affairs.

Mill, J.S. (1861/1985) *Utilitarianism*. New York: Macmillan.

Mishra, P. (2012) *From the ruins of empire: The revolt against the west and the making of Asia*. London: Penguin.

Mourshed, M., Chijioke, C., & Barber, M. (2010) *How the world's most improved school systems keep getting better*. London: McKinsey & Company.

OECD (2010) *Strong performers and successful reformers: Lessons from PISA for the United States*. Paris: OECD.

OECD (2014) *TALIS 2013 results: An international perspective on teaching and learning*. Paris: OECD.

OECD (2012) *PISA 2012 results: What makes schools successful? Resources, policies and practices, volume 4*. Paris: OECD.

Otto, J., & Spiewak, M. (2016, February 25) Nie mehr allein [Never again alone]. *Die Zeit*, p. 62.

Richter, D., & Pant, H.A. (2016) *Lehrerkooperation in Deutschland* [Teacher cooperation in Germany]. Gütersloh, Germany: Bertelsmann Foundation.

Schleicher, A. (2016) *Teaching excellence through professional learning and policy reform: Lessons from around the world.* Paris: OECD.

Shirley, D., & MacDonald, E. (2016) *The mindful teacher.* New York: Teachers College Press.

Skerrett, A. (2015) *Teaching transnational youth: Literacy and education in a changing world.* New York: Teachers College Press.

Tan, C. (2013) *Learning from Shanghai: Lessons on achieving educational success.* Dordrecht, Holland: Springer.

Tucker, M.S. (Ed.) (2011) *Surpassing Shanghai: An agenda for American education built on the world's leading systems.* Cambridge, MA: Harvard Education Press.

UNICEF (2013) *Child well-being in rich countries: A comparative overview.* Florence: Innocenti.

Zhao, Y. (2014) *Who's afraid of the big bad dragon? Why China has the best (and worst) education system in the world.* San Francisco: Jossey-Bass.

2

THE EVIDENTIARY IMPERATIVE

STUDYING RESULTS

Pasi Sahlberg[1] is to be credited with the acronym "GERM," which stands for the "Global Educational Reform Movement." The GERM has been the reigning ideology in many schools and systems under the old imperatives. It has five components:

1   the standardization of learning and teaching;
2   emphasis on numeracy and literacy to the neglect of other subjects;
3   curricular prescription;
4   marketplace models of reform; and
5   accountability and surveillance through testing.

Sahlberg explains that the GERM "is not a formal global policy program, but rather an unofficial agenda that relies on a certain set of assumptions to improve education systems."[2] This makes it difficult, but also important, to document.

Although the GERM is a humorous acronym, in some ways it is also a misleading one. By using a biological metaphor, the term mystifies social processes. The GERM moniker makes it appear that educational change spreads like a bacterium or a virus. It obscures the role of power and values in driving change forward. The GERM slogan makes it seem as if one widespread model of education in the world today is the result of a social movement, like the civil rights, environmental, or women's rights movements. These social movements were grassroots, bottom-up campaigns. They share no similarities with the ways in which the GERM has spread and become institutionalized.

Regardless of these issues, the public good has been served by the acronym of the GERM because it has helped to identify the theory of action that was passed into laws such as the No Child Left Behind Act and the Race to the Top in the United States, the National Literacy and Numeracy Strategy in England, and market-based reforms in Sweden. In each case, something called New Public Management (NPM) has been applied to education. NPM brought competition into the public sector with the goal of lowering costs, expanding choice, and increasing efficiencies. "NPM is no longer new," according to one account that is itself a decade old.[3] "Rather it is a two-decades old set of public management ideas" that have gone mainstream.[4]

The ideology of NPM originated in England during the administration of Prime Minister Margaret Thatcher in the 1980s. With the collapse of the Soviet Union and the end of the Cold War, it appeared to many that collectivist solutions to social problems had been proven ineffective. Policy makers embraced NPM to rectify what they viewed as unresponsive government bureaucracies. NPM reforms were adapted rapidly by Sweden and by Commonwealth nations such as Australia and New Zealand. In the US, former bastions of welfare-state liberalism such as the Brookings Institution began promoting scholars such as John Chubb and Terry Moe who advocated the ideology of NPM in education.[5] Margaret Thatcher had a personal friendship with Chilean military dictator Augusto Pinochet, and Chile became one of the first countries to bring NPM to the reform of its public school system.[6]

In its first years, NPM appealed to many who were seeking to promote innovation in government. Even many traditional advocates of an older welfare state model were eventually won over by NPM reformers. They recreated themselves as *New* Labour in England and *New* Democrats in the US. There was genuine excitement during this time, with policy makers and public intellectuals seeking new ways to open up government and to make it more accountable.

But as soon as NPM education policies were put into place, problems surfaced. Governments contracted out services to private or semi-private providers, but subsequently found that they were no longer able to direct what was happening in schools so easily. If disaffected parents wanted to hold school systems accountable for poor student outcomes, squabbles ensued between the educational management organizations that now ran the schools and districts that still funded them. Those students who presented behavioral challenges or who had learning disabilities became those least desired by schools that were now competing against one another for the best test scores.

NPM made teacher union organizing more difficult. This yielded short-term benefits to governments in terms of reducing costs, but a decline in labor union density is also correlated with the shrinkage of the middle classes and the growth of economic inequality.[7] Having the opportunity to choose among service providers sounds positive, but has little meaning for many people who cannot understand the choices because they lack formal education, are unfamiliar with how to discriminate amongst providers, or are confronted by language barriers.

The ideology of NPM, when applied to education through the GERM, can sound attractive to students and parents because it promises freedom and innovation. In practice, however, markets called for greater standardization for quality control purposes. Because not everything can or should be tested, some subjects such as mathematics and literacy have been exalted over social studies, science, the arts, physical education, and foreign languages. Even within the basics, some skills, and not necessarily the most important ones, were privileged over others because they were more utilitarian.

English and language arts classes increasingly came to abandon the reading of fiction for the comprehension of factual texts. Problem solving has been sacrificed for memorization, and synthesis for information processing. Those things that are the easiest to test, involving memorization or computation, are emphasized. Those that are the most difficult to measure, entailing the ability to look at complex problems from multiple points of view to reach an independent interpretation, are neglected.

So NPM isn't a virus or an infection—it is a very deliberate invention that has become institutionalized and disseminated. NPM is not a random plague, but an ideology and a set of strategies used against older styles of social democracy with strong welfare states and high degrees of public investment and union protection. These ideas are spread by political leaders, think tanks, for-profit corporations, and a variety of their supporters, who share ideas at high levels. They then try them out back home based on their own interests. Once it has been set in place, the internal logic of the NPM spreads out the ideology even further.

NPM has its intellectual as well as political advocates. High priests of the free market include such intellectual authorities as Ayn Rand, Friedrich von Hayek, Ludwig von Mises, and Milton Friedman.[8] They viewed themselves as champions of freedom in a century of political totalitarianism. They saw markets as the most important way to temper the tendency of governments to augment their power. Better outcomes would result, it was believed, through competition and decentralization.

But has the ideology of NPM led to improved outcomes in practice?

The three countries that have been most resolute at pushing through NPM in education have been England, Sweden, and the US. These are developed countries that are policy trendsetters not only in their own regions but also around the world. Their educational leaders have been in frequent interaction with one another over recent years and they have exhibited many forms of policy borrowing on matters from teacher preparation, professional development, and accountability systems.

As Figure 2.1 shows, the PISA results of England and Sweden in mathematics have fallen from above average to average or below average from 2000 to 2012, precipitously in each case. US results also have fallen, although they began at a lower level and have not declined so dramatically.[9]

Are the patterns that are apparent for mathematics also true for reading and science? If so, then it most likely is not the result of a single curricular subject and how it is taught. It must be the manifestation of a deeper pattern that has to do with how a given ideology and its affiliated policies impact student achievement. Here are the data for the same nations in Figures 2.2 and 2.3 in reading and science.

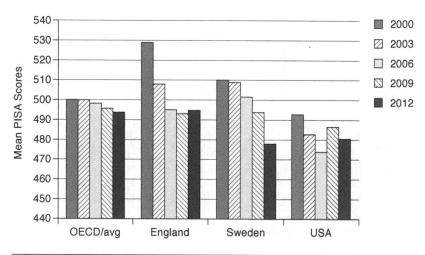

Figure 2.1 PISA Math Scores for the OECD, England, Sweden, and the US, 2000–2012.

Figures 2.1–2.3 reveal a similar pattern of declines for England and Sweden, and fluctuations or slight declines for the US. That there are these evident similarities regardless of the subject areas suggests that it is imprudent to attribute results to a given curricula or to teachers' preparation in one discipline or another. If this were the case one would see gains in reading, and declines in science, for

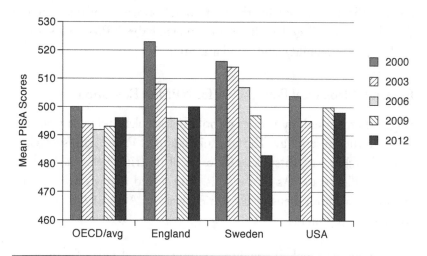

Figure 2.2 PISA Reading Scores for the OECD, England, Sweden, and the US, 2000–2012 (PISA 2006 results for the US are not available due to sampling errors).

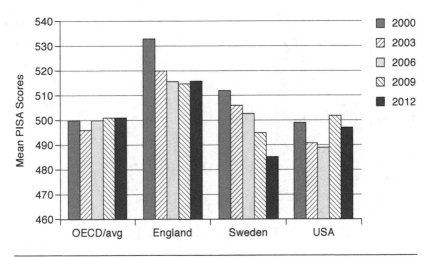

Figure 2.3 PISA Science Scores for the OECD, England, Sweden, and the US, 2000–2012.

example. Since this is not the case, it is more likely that broader factors, including policies, have shaped these results.

The policies in question belong to an *ideological imperative*. This is a deliberately developed theory of educational change that has been transported across countries by actors and interest groups with similar political commitments. They have been well organized and supported by governments, research institutions, and assorted hangers-on who, in some cases, have built highly successful careers by advocating not only for the efficacy, but also for the high moral principles of freedom and choice that are alleged to have accompanied the NPM strategies of markets, accountability, and standardization.

England: Ideological Powerhouse for NPM in Education

England embarked on a series of bold marketplace reforms from the 1980s to the present day. The administration of Prime Minister Margaret Thatcher was outspoken in terms of its criticisms of all sectors of the welfare state. As part of this it advanced a brash new agenda by passing a comprehensive Education Reform Act in 1988. This had six major components:

1　A new national curriculum, emphasizing England's imperial legacy as a world leader.

2 New systems of accountability for student outcomes and control of the profession, enhancing greater prescription from above.

3 Mechanisms for identifying poorly performing teachers and failing schools, empowering government to close such schools.

4 Increased parent choice in selecting their child's school from a greater array of options within a diverse provider model.

5 A transfer of funding from Local Education Authorities (the equivalent of US school districts) to schools themselves, removing intermediary supports and coordination.

6 The empowerment of school principals ("headteachers" in England) and governors (volunteers who help to run the school).[10]

A quarter century after the Reform Act was launched, what do we know about subsequent educational outcomes?

In the Global Index of Cognitive Skills and Educational Attainment published in 2012 and 2014, the United Kingdom was ranked as having the sixth best education system in the world.[11] This index was developed by the Economist Intelligence Unit and published by Pearson, the world's largest for-profit education company. It presents a favorable view of educational performance in the UK and an apparent vindication of NPM. However, unlike other indices of educational performance, the Pearson index includes higher education in the metric, so the elite universities at Oxford and Cambridge raise the scores by being added to the mix. Second, the indicators on the Pearson index are drawn from the UK as a whole, while NPM took root less strongly in Wales, Scotland, and Northern Ireland than in England in education. Last, it is worth observing that the Chief Education Adviser for Pearson, Sir Michael Barber, was responsible for England's change ideology and its affiliated policies under the Tony Blair government. For Pearson to succeed with its global business reach, it hardly is helpful if its Chief Education Adviser prevailed over policies that led to problematic outcomes on international large-scale assessments.

Among measures that apply to school performance only, England did far less well than on the Pearson index. The TIMSS 2011 and PIRLS 2011 studies investigated the results of grade 4 and grade 8 students internationally and disaggregated the nations of the UK separately. England's results for reading, math, and science were improving but did not place it in a class of global leaders.[12]

Meanwhile, on OECD's PISA tests that measure how students apply their knowledge to real-world problems, England fell from the first administration of the test in 2000. The declines cut across the three tested areas of literacy, mathematics, and science. The results suggest that something in policy or society is responsible for the decline, rather than anything specific to one subject or skill area.

With the rise in and disruptive effects of markets, free schools and academy chains, as well as standardization and testing, England's results declined on PISA, and social segregation by class was exacerbated. This occurred in spite of a positive ranking of English teachers for professionalism on the OECD's TALIS.[13] The problems in English schools originate from policy, not from the profession. When English educators have had opportunities to contest the competitive ideology and to collaborate across jurisdictions, they have posted positive results in London and Manchester.[14] But this is a very different model of change than that prescribed from above.

England provides a fascinating case of a government resolutely pushing forward with a hardened *ideological imperative* even when evidence points out overwhelming problems with the strategy. The government is able to persist in its approach by avoiding language that refers to commercialization and privatization. Instead, the official rhetoric promotes freedom, autonomy, and choice. Such language has innate appeal. But it masks pernicious consequences.

English educators and parent advocacy groups have challenged the spread of academies and free schools but thus far have been unable to prevail. One unintended consequence is that teachers are leaving the profession, with an 85 percent shortage of teacher candidates in some subject areas.[15] Even in subject areas where teacher education programs prepare large numbers of student teachers, increasing numbers of graduates are opting to teach in Commonwealth nations such as Australia and Canada where working conditions and student achievement results are better.[16] Instead of reversing policy, the government is adapting by recruiting teachers from countries such as Jamaica, where teachers make salaries at one-fifth of the English pay scale.[17] With tentative legal status in England, such teachers are unlikely to lead a principled resistance to government policies.

The current reform model in England is perfecting unsustainable change. The integrity of the profession has been eroded, and English students' results on PISA show significant declines from one test administration to the next. Young teachers are observing the declining morale, enforced competitiveness, and increasing surveillance, and are opting out. It is hard to imagine a dramatic turnaround of student learning results in such an environment.

Sweden: A Pre-Emptive Strike and its Educational Free-Fall

At the beginning of the new millennium, international educators streamed to Sweden to learn what had been done to achieve its first admirable results on PISA in 2001. At the time no one would have anticipated that Sweden would go on to experience the largest drop in mathematics on PISA of any nation in subsequent years.[18] No one foresaw that the literacy and science results on PISA also would plummet downward. Swedes are known for their generous social provision, gender equity, and economic prosperity. Since international rankings began, Sweden has been at or near the top of international indicators on child well-being.[19] So, what happened?

Sweden's struggles are especially acute because it has to suffer the indignity of knowing that its former colony, Finland, has became a global poster-child of school improvement, hosting over 2,500 educational visitors a year.[20] (In spite of what some Finns proclaim about their cooperative culture, Finns agree that placing ahead of Sweden has been enormously gratifying.) Like Finland, Sweden has undertaken ambitious educational reforms in past decades, but the Finns have emphasized equity and professionalism, while Swedish policy makers have embraced markets, with different PISA results as a consequence. No wonder Swedish educators have some of the lowest morale of any educators in any nation, according to the OECD in its 2013 TALIS study.[21] Only 5 percent of Swedish teachers believed that teaching is "a valued profession in society," compared with 59 percent of teachers in Finland.[22]

It has been a shock for the Swedes. For decades, Sweden seemed to have it all: spectacular social benefits, generous private philanthropy, genuine gender equity, and magnificent prosperity. When German educators and policy makers saw how well Sweden did on the first PISA results in 2000 they organized school visits north to cities such as Stockholm, Helsingborg, and Gothenburg to explore reforms that they might adapt to their own contexts. So how has it come to pass that the Swedish educational model became so flawed when so many of the other aspects of this Scandinavian society have been such sparkling triumphs?

The driving force in the Swedish case was political. Neoclassical economists who endorsed the principles of NPM persuaded policy makers to bring the principles of marketplace competition to public institutions. They hoped that by providing greater choice and efficiency to citizens they would be able to restore public confidence in government, a precondition for the provision of badly needed revenues for everything from city services to public schools. Swedish school reforms adapted from English predecessors began in the 1990s and then increased further in 2006 with greater government encouragement of what are called "free schools" that are similar to charters in the US and academies in England. The traditional Scandinavian emphasis upon "a school for all" was supplanted by policy imperatives upholding more parent and student school choice in a diverse provider model.[23]

Swedish reforms were introduced by the Social Democrats who had been the primary architects of that nation's modern welfare state in the first place. Following public opinion surveys indicating voter dissatisfaction with education, the Social Democrats sought to circumvent a conservative electoral victory by adapting the new NPM strategies that had been promulgated in England. Some of the themes of England's Education Reform Act—a shared national curriculum, accountability for the profession, greater parental empowerment at the local level—all fit into traditional Nordic values respecting the rights of the individual, the responsibilities of the public sector, and a shared curricular understanding of what matters and why. This helps us to understand why it is that the adaptation to the GERM in Sweden provoked little resistance, even as declines in achievement accelerated.

In the Swedish variation of NPM in education, private-equity firms have been authorized to run schools to draw on public revenues to reap profits. In Sweden, parents are not charged tuition for school providers, even if they are essentially private schools. The Swedish government has embraced an even more laissez-faire approach than England. Parents have been free to choose whichever school they believe will be best for their children, without transparency of results through testing.

In 1991 Sweden had only 60 free schools that were not part of the public sector, but by 2010 this number had risen to 709.[24] Teachers' working conditions have declined because they are less able to raise criticisms that could lead to improvements when they are in schools that treat them as if they are working for private companies.[25] Swedish reforms have been expensive to implement and they have contributed to a sharp rise in inequality of educational outcomes.[26]

Champions of NPM in Swedish schools uphold the promise of the model in spite of the declining PISA results. Economist Tino Sanandaji, writing in *National Review*, argued that "the reform worked" because "parents and pupils in private schools tend to be more satisfied than average."[27] Sanandaji cites one survey that revealed "67 percent of the Swedish public wants to retain school choice, including 59 percent of Social Democratic voters."[28] The culprits for the Swedish PISA results, according to Sanandaji, are the decline of homework, liberality in allowing students to bring mobile phones to class, and a high percentage of students who are tardy. Swedish teachers have comparatively low salaries and their students receive less contact time with their instructors, Sanandaji contends. The way that teachers inflate grades to make their schools attractive to students and parents, he says, needs to be checked through better accountability.

Economist Gabriel Heller Sahlgren, writing for the Friedman Foundation for Educational Choice, further extended Sandaji's interpretation.[29] Sahlgren referenced research by Anders Böhlmark and Mikael Lidahl that found "short-term positive effects on test scores and grades, as well as on long-term outcomes in upper-secondary school and university credits," for students that enrolled in the new free schools rather than traditional public schools.[30] Arguing that

"All competition is simply not equal," Sahlgren contended that "there is very little evidence of any negative effects of choice or competition on education quality."[31] Sweden's declining results should be attributed to design flaws such as the poor interface between decentralized schools and centralized university admissions rather than any inherent problems with marketplace models, according to this perspective.

The final straw for many Swedes occurred in 2013 when JB Education, a provider owned by a Danish private equity firm, declared bankruptcy and closed its doors. This left 11,000 students displaced and over 1,000 staff unemployed. Students of markets know that business failure should be expected, but policy makers in Sweden were taken by surprise with this turn of events. Students and parents had to start from scratch in selecting new schools. At the same time refugees from war in the Middle East began arriving in Sweden in large numbers. Instead of providing stability for the newcomers, the education sector was in tumult.

This policy-induced disruption in the lives of learners, along with the volatility of the labor market for educators, created a consensus for change in Sweden. In September 2014 the pro-market governing coalition was voted out of power and replaced by a left-of-center coalition that is trying to reverse Sweden's educational trajectory. The new government has put together a commission consisting of academic experts, school leaders, teacher union representatives, and classroom teachers to guide new reforms. It is exploring measures such as preventing free schools from making a profit, mandating the boards of such schools to be gender equitable with a view to moderating the primacy of market concerns, and rebuilding the teaching profession by investing in teacher leadership. Although it is too early to say what policy reforms will ensue, an anachronistic *ideological imperative* for markets and choice in the public sector has come under intense scrutiny.

The United States: A Change of Course

For many years of the past quarter century it has not mattered which party has been in power in England or Sweden. When it came to education policy there has been consensus across governments. Policy leaders know that their publics are anxious and seek reassurance about the future. While schools have little or no impact on business cycles per se, they do contribute to the human capital available to societies for economic growth. Given the limited time that politicians have to demonstrate results, it is hardly surprising that they place enormous pressure on schools to measure results and then lift performance. The same trend lines have been visible in the US, with scarcely any distinctions between Democrats and Republicans on education policy.

Major upheavals within political parties have supported this shift. New Labour in England and the Democrats for Education Reform in the US developed in tandem away from an emphasis on the welfare state and toward the programmatic agenda of the five old imperatives. The GERM ideology spread through political allegiances and the adoption of new strategies. New Labour and the Democrats took political risks along the way that alienated teachers' unions. This estrangement in England led to a unanimous vote of no confidence in Education Secretary Michael Gove in 2013. US educators passed a similar resolution when the National Education Association (NEA) called for the resignation of Secretary of Education Arne Duncan on July 4, 2014. Their protest worked, although not immediately. By December 2015 he was gone.

In the same month, President Obama signed into law the Every Student Succeeds Act (ESSA). This decisively repudiated many of the most ideologically charged components of the now utterly discredited No Child Left Behind Act. Gone was the hated Adequate Yearly Progress report to the federal government that led to micromanaging of districts from Washington, DC. Gone was the federal requirement to tie teacher evaluations to student achievement, which unfairly punished those teachers who bravely took on the most oppositional and alienated of students in hope of bringing them back into the fold. Gone was the requirement that school districts identify those who were described as unqualified teachers, which in practice meant that in rural schools almost every secondary educator was unqualified because in small schools, teachers had to teach outside of their subject areas. Gone was the federal requirement that school districts provide school choice, which often favored start-up charter schools with no track records of success, when the local neighbor-hood school was struggling. To top it all off, the new Secretary of Education, John King, apologized to the nation's teachers for the tone of disrespect that had often emanated from the US Department of Education in previous years.

What led to the dramatic change of course? A dose of *Realpolitik* is helpful here. The Democrats had alienated their traditional allies in the National Education Association (NEA) and the American Federation of Teachers (AFT). For their part, conservative critics were correct that the government had violated Article X of the US Constitution, which allocates educational matters to the states. With elections upcoming in November 2016 a rare bipartisan consensus was achieved. No Child Left Behind and the ideology behind it became a matter for the history books.

Or at least that could be the case. The ESSA still requires states to administer standardized tests in math and reading in grades 3–8 and once in high school, which still is much more testing than in many other nations. While federal policies promoting marketplace models have been cut back under ESSA, nothing prevents these from being maintained or even expanded upon by the states.

More seriously, it could take years for US education to recover from the turbulence that the *ideological imperative* and its affiliated policies spread throughout the system. Teacher turnover now occurs at a startling speed. In 2008 the modal teacher in the US was a rookie in her or his first year of teaching.[32] About 13 percent of the country's 3.4 million teachers either leave the profession each year or switch schools.[33] These disruptions cost the country between $1 billion and $2.2 billion annually.[34] New research is revealing that, contrary to popular opinion, teachers need years to become experts in teaching, and that they continue to improve throughout their careers.[35] Schools need diverse staff to optimize the learning experi-ence of all, and this includes teachers with a diverse range of years in the profession.

For these reasons stabilizing the profession must now be the first order of business for educational leaders in the US. How can this be done? Increasingly, a growing body of research points the way. Consolidate educators' professional knowledge base. Encourage collegiality through their supportive peer networks that break through norms of isolation in the classroom. Develop decisional capital. These are themes to which we shall return in Chapter 4 when we address the *professional imperative*.

The Evidentiary Imperative

In recent years there has been a massive backlash against the PISA tests. Yong Zhao, for example, has accused Andreas Schleicher, Director for the Director of Education and Skills at the OECD, of promoting "romanticized misery" and "glorified authoritarianism" because of Schleicher's enthusiasm for top-ranking Shanghai.[36] Richard Münch denounced PISA, along with McKinsey & Company, for "the transformation of all parts of life according to economic models."[37] More than 200 educators from around the world, many of them prominent researchers, signed a petition in 2014 arguing that PISA was "dangerously narrowing our collective imagination regarding what education is and ought to be about."[38]

These are serious criticisms of PISA and should be read carefully. To a certain extent the OECD has brought them upon itself by failing to bring a properly scientific attitude to its work. OECD publications are filled with references to other OECD publications, none of which go through the ordinary process of peer review. This is out of proportion to their actual contribution to contemporary scholarship. Even when scholars come together in an attitude of fastidious objectivity, as did an international team under the leadership of Stefan Hopmann, Gertrude Brinke, and Martin Retzl, their contributions have been completely overlooked in subsequent OECD publications.[39] This naturally builds resentments amongst those who could contribute to research on international comparisons of student learning results.

Having said that, it is also important to note that the majority of criticisms of PISA have to do with policy-related interpretations of the results rather than the technical standards of the tests themselves. This is more difficult terrain for critics because there is good evidence that the OECD maintains rigorous standards with the PISA tests. As the gap in Figure 2.2 above revealed, when the US did not meet sampling requirements for reading, its results were disqualified. All of the English results for 2003 were disqualified as well. The bars for mathematics, reading, and science in Figures 2.1, 2.2, and 2.3 are all taken from an independent analysis conducted by John Mickewright and Sylvke Schnepft.[40] They produced a persuasive argument that the OECD was "overly cautious"[41] in excluding the English data because of alleged response bias. Here the argument is not that the OECD's technical standards are too weak, but that they are too high.

Educators, like all professionals, must submit to an *evidentiary imperative*. So let us study PISA results to see what they can tell us, not as a dogma imposed from above, but as a resource that can supplement our observations of students' learning. Let's be open-minded and learn from whatever evidence we find that is available. When trend lines are clear, let's ask after anachronistic ideologies that we may be operating with and submit them to fresh scrutiny.

At the same time, it is possible to agree with some critics that the OECD has occasionally gone beyond what the data reveal in its policy recommendations. Some of its recommendations have in fact contributed to the spread of the GERM. To understand how this occurred, we need to uncover a tacit *imperial imperative* that has undermined a promising future for educational change.

Notes

1   Sahlberg, P. (2011) *Finnish lessons: What can the world can learn from educational change in Finland?* New York: Teachers College Press, p. 99.
2   Sahlberg, *Finnish lessons*, p. 99.
3   Dunleavy, P., Margetts, H., Bastow, S., & Tinkler, J. (2005) *New public management is dead: Long live digital era governance.* London: EDS Innovation Research Programme, p. 4.
4   Dunleavy et al., *New public management is dead*, p. 4.
5   Chubb, J.E., & Moe, T.M. (1990) *Politics, markets, and America's schools.* Washington, DC: Brookings Institution.
6   Bellei, C. (2015) *El gran experimento: Mercado y privatización del la educación chilena* [The big experiment: Markets and the privatization of Chilean education]. Santiago: LOM.
7   Noah, T. (2012) *The great divergence: America's growing inequality crisis and what we can do about it.* New York: Bloomsbury Press.
8   See Rand, A. (1943) *The fountainhead*. Indianapolis, IN: Bobbs Merrill; Hayek, F. (1976) *The road to serfdom*. Chicago: University of Chicago Press; Mises, L. (1949) *Human action: A treatise on economics*. New Haven: Yale University Press; and Friedman, M. (1962) *Capitalism and freedom*. Chicago: University of Chicago Press.

9 The tables presenting PISA data in Chapters 2 and 3 of this book are compiled from OECD data supplemented with other sources that are explained below. 2000 data for the OCED average, Sweden, the US, and Germany are taken from the National Center for Education Statistics (2002) *Highlights from the 2000 Program for International Student Assessment of the Program for International Student Assessment (PISA)*. Washington, DC: US Department of Education, pp. 4, 9. 2000 data for England are taken from Gill, B., Dunn, M., & Goddard, E. (2002) *Student achievement in England: Results in reading, mathematical and scientific literacy among 15 year olds from OECD PISA 2000 study*. London: Social Survey Division of the Office for National Statistics, pp. 28, 43, 53. 2003 data for the OECD average, Sweden, the US, and Germany are taken from OECD (2004) *Learning for tomorrow's world—First results from PISA 2003*. Paris: OECD, pp. 45, 273, 281, 294. English data were not included in *Learning for tomorrow's world* because the OECD determined that the United Kingdom did not meet its technical standards for PISA 2003. Researchers at the Southampton Statistical Sciences Research Institute have advanced a persuasive argument that the English data are trustworthy, and those numbers are reported here. See Micklewright, J., & Schnepf, S.V. (2006) *Response bias in England in PISA 2000 and 2003*. London: Department for Education and Skills, pp. 56, 59. 2006 data for the OECD average, Sweden, the US, and Germany are taken from OECD (2007) *Science competencies for tomorrow's world-Executive summary*. Paris: OECD, pp. 22, 47, 48, 53. English data are taken from Bradshaw, J., Sturman, L., Vappula, H., Ager, R., & Wheater, R. (2007) *Achievement of 15-year-olds in England: PISA 2006 National Report*. London: Department for Children, Schools, and Families, pp. 19, 28, 33. The US did not meet OECD technical requirements for reading in 2006. 2009 data for the OECD average, Sweden, the US, and Germany are taken from OECD (2010) *PISA 2009 results: Executive summary*. Paris: OECD, p. 8. English data are taken from Bradshaw, J., Ager, R., Burge, B., & Wheater, R. (2010) *PISA 2009: Achievement of 15-year-olds in England*. London: National Foundation for Educational Research, pp. 26, 29, 32. 2012 data for the OECD average, Sweden, the US, and Germany are taken from OECD (2014) *PISA 2012 results in focus: What 15-year-olds know and what they can do with what they know*. Paris: OECD, p. 5. English results are taken from OECD (2014) *Country notes, Programme for International Student Assessment (PISA) Results from PISA 2012: United Kingdom*. Paris: OECD, pp. 2–3.

10 Parliament (1988) *Education Reform Act 1988*. London: Her Majesty's Stationery Office. Retrieved from www.legislation.gov.uk/ukpga/1988/40/pdfs/ukpga_19880040_en.pdf.

11 Kielstra, P. (2012) *The learning curve: Lessons in country performance in education. 2012 report*. London: Pearson.

12 See Mullis, I.V.S., Martin, M.O., Foy, P., & Drucker, K.T. (2012) *PIRLS 2011 international results in reading*. Chestnut Hill, MA: TIMSS & PIRLS International Study Center, Lynch School of Education, Boston College; Mullis, I.V.S., Martin, M.O., Foy, P., & Arora, A. (2012) *TIMSS 2011 international results in mathematics*. Chestnut Hill, MA: TIMSS & PIRLS International Study Center, Lynch School of Education, Boston College; Martin, M.O., Mullis, I.V.S., Foy, P., & Stanco, G.M. (2012) *TIMSS 2011 international results in science*. TIMSS & PIRLS International Study Center, Lynch School of Education, Boston College.

13 Schleicher, A. (2016) *Teaching excellence through professional learning and policy reform: Lessons from around the world*. Paris: OECD, p. 39.

14 Ainscow, M. (2015) *Towards self-improving school systems: Lessons from a city challenge*. New York: Routledge.

15 Doward, J. (2015, December 26) Schools in crisis as graduates turn their backs on teaching. *Guardian*. Retrieved from www.theguardian.com/uk-news/2015/dec/26/teacher-shortage-graduates.

16 Weale, S. (2016, February 26) UK schools suffering as newly qualified teachers "flock abroad." *Guardian*. Retrieved from www.theguardian.com/education/2016/feb/26/uk-schools-suffering-as-new-teachers-flock-abroad-warns-chief-inspector.

17 Boffey, D. (2015, October 10) Dozens of Jamaican teachers hired to work in British schools. *Guardian*. Retrieved from www.theguardian.com/education/2015/oct/11/agency-hires-jamaican-teachers-for-english-schools.

18 OECD (2015) *Improving schools in Sweden: An OECD perspective*. Paris: OECD.

19 UNICEF (2013) *Child well-being in rich countries: A comparative overview*. Florence: Innocenti.

20 OECD (2014) *TALIS 2013 results: An international perspective on teaching and learning*. Paris: OECD, p. 187.

21 OECD, *TALIS 2013 results*, p. 187.

22 OECD (2014) *Country note: Sweden results from TALIS 2013*. Paris: OECD, p. 1.

23 Astrand, B. (2016) From citizens into consumers: The transformation of democratic ideals into school markets in Sweden. In: Adamson, F., Åstrand, B., & Darling-Hammond, L. (Eds.) *Global education reform: How privatization and public investment influence education outcomes*. New York: Routledge, pp. 73–109. Sanandaji, T. (2014, July 21) Sweden has an education crisis, but it wasn't caused by school choice. *National Review Online*. Retrieved from www.nationalreview.com/agenda/383304/sweden-has-education-crisis-it-wasnt-caused-school-choice-tino-sanandaji?target=author&tid=902932. Blossing, U., Imsen, G., & Moos, L. (2014) *The Nordic education model: "A school for all" encounters neo-liberal policy*. Dordrecht, Holland: Springer.

24 Wiborg, S. (2010) *Swedish free schools: Do they work?* London: Centre for Learning and Life Chances in Knowledge Economies and Societies, Institute of Education, University of London.

25 Arreman, I.E., & Holm, A.S. (2011) Privatisation of public education? The mergence of independent upper secondary schools in Sweden. *Journal of Educational Policy* 26(2), 225–243.

26 OECD, *Improving schools in Sweden*.

27 Sanandaji, Sweden has an education crisis, p. 3.

28 Sanandaji, Sweden has an education crisis, p. 3.

29 Sahlgren, G.H. (2014, July 23) Is Swedish school choice disastrous—Or is the reading of the evidence? Retrieved from www.edchoice.org/is-swedish-school-choice-disastrous-or-is-the-reading-of-the-evidence/.

30 Sahlgren, Is Swedish school choice disastrous—Or is the reading of the evidence?, p. 1. Böhlmark, A., & Lindahl, M. (2013) *Independent schools and long-run educational outcomes—Evidence from Sweden's large scale voucher reform*. Stockholm: Swedish Institute for Social Research, Stockholm University.

31 Sahlgren, Is Swedish school choice disastrous—Or is the reading of the evidence?, p. 5.

32 Ingersoll, R., Merrill, L., & Stuckey, D. (2014) *Seven trends: The transformation of the teaching force*. Philadelphia: Consortium for Policy Research in Education, University of Pennsylvania.

33 Alliance for Excellent Education (2014) *On the path to equity: Improving the effectiveness of beginning teachers*. Washington, DC: Alliance for Excellent Education.

34 Alliance for Excellent Education, *On the path to equity*.

35 Two recent studies challenge prevailing opinions about teachers' expertise leveling off after their first few years of teaching. The first is Papay, J.P., & Kraft, M.A. (2014) Productivity returns to experience in the teacher labor market: Methodological

challenges and new evidence on long-term career improvement. Providence, RI: authors. Retrieved from http://scholar.harvard.edu/files/mkraft/files/jpubec_-_returns_to_experience_manuscript_-_r2.pdf. The second is Ladd, H.F., & Soresen, L.C. (2015) *Returns to teacher experience: Student achievement and motivation in middle school.* Washington, DC: American Institutes of Research.
36 Zhao, Y. (2014) *Who's afraid of the big bad dragon? Why China has the best (and worst) education system in the world.* San Francisco: Jossey-Bass, p. 7.
37 Münch, R. (2008) *Globale Eliten, Lokale Autoritäten: Politik unter dem Regime von PISA, McKinsey, & Co.* [Global elites, local authorities: Politics in the regime of PISA and McKinsey & Company]. Frankfurt: Suhrkamp Verlag, p. 7.
38 Retrieved from www.theguardian.com/education/2014/may/06/oecd-pisa-tests-damaging-education-academics.
39 Hopmann, S., Brinke, G., & Retzl, M. (2007) *PISA zufolge PISA: PISA according to PISA.* Berlin: LIT Verlag.
40 Micklewright & Schnepf, *Response bias.*
41 Micklewright & Schnepf, *Response bias,* p. 61.

References

Ainscow, M. (2015) *Towards self-improving school systems: Lessons from a city challenge.* New York: Routledge.

Alliance for Excellent Education (2014) *On the path to equity: Improving the effectiveness of beginning teachers.* Washington, DC: Alliance for Excellent Education.

Arreman, I.E., & Holm, A.S. (2011) Privatisation of public education? The mergence of independent upper secondary schools in Sweden. *Journal of Educational Policy* 26(2), 225–243.

Åstrand, B. (2016) From citizens into consumers: The transformation of democratic ideals into school markets in Sweden. In: Adamson, A., Astrand, B., & Darling-Hammond, L. (Eds.) *Global education reform: How privatization and public investment influence education outcomes.* New York: Routledge, pp. 73–109.

Bellei, C. (2015) *El gran experimento: Mercado y privatización del la educación chilena* [The big experiment: Markets and the privatization of Chilean education]. Santiago: LOM.

Blossing, U., Imsen, G., & Moos, L. (2014) *The Nordic education model: "A school for all" encounters neo-liberal policy.* Dordrecht, Holland: Springer.

Boffey, D. (2015, October 10) Dozens of Jamaican teachers hired to work in British schools. *Guardian.* Retrieved from www.theguardian.com/education/2015/oct/11/agency-hires-jamaican-teachers-for-english-schools.

Böhlmark, A., & Lindahl, M. (2013) *Independent schools and long-run educational outcomes—Evidence from Sweden's large scale voucher reform.* Stockholm: Swedish Institute for Social Research, Stockholm University.

Bradshaw, J., Sturman, L., Vappula, H., Ager, R., & Wheater, R. (2007) *Achievement of 15-year-olds in England: PISA 2006 National Report.* London: Department for Children, Schools, and Families.

Bradshaw, J., Ager, R., Burge, B., & Wheater, R. (2010) *PISA 2009: Achieve-ment of 15-year-olds in England*. London: National Foundation for Educational Research.

Chubb, J.E., & Moe, T.M. (1990) *Politics, markets, and America's schools*. Washington, DC: Brookings Institution.

Doward, J. (2015, December 26) Schools in crisis as graduates turn their backs on teaching. *Guardian*. Retrieved from www.theguardian.com/uk-news/2015/dec/26/teacher-shortage-graduates.

Dunleavy, P., Margetts, H., Bastow, S., & Tinkler, J. (2005) *New public man-agement is dead: Long live digital era governance*. London: EDS Innova-tion Research Programme.

Friedman, M. (1962) *Capitalism and freedom*. Chicago: University of Chicago Press.

Gill, B., Dunn, M. & Goddard, E. (2002) *Student achievement in England: Results in reading, mathematical and scientific literacy among 15 year olds from OECD PISA 2000 study*. London: Social Survey Division of the Office for National Statistics.

Hayek, F. (1976) *The road to serfdom*. Chicago: University of Chicago Press.

Hopmann, S., Brinke, G., & Retzl, M. (2007) *PISA zufolge PISA: PISA according to PISA*. Berlin: LIT Verlag.

Ingersoll, R., Merrill, L., & Stuckey, D. (2014) *Seven trends: The transforma-tion of the teaching force*. Philadelphia: Consortium for Policy Research in Education, University of Pennsylvania.

Kielstra, P. (2012) *The learning curve: Lessons in country performance in educa-tion. 2012 report*. London: Pearson.

Ladd, H.F., & Soresen, L.C. (2015) *Returns to teacher experience: Student achievement and motivation in middle school*. Washington, DC: Amer-ican Institutes of Research.

Martin, M.O., Mullis, I.V.S., Foy, P., & Stanco, G.M. (2012) *TIMSS 2011 international results in science*. TIMSS & PIRLS International Study Center, Lynch School of Education, Boston College.

Micklewright, J., & Schnepf, S.V. (2006) *Response bias in England in PISA 2000 and 2003*. London: Department for Education and Skills.

Mises, L. (1949) *Human action: A treatise on economics*. New Haven: Yale Uni-versity Press.

Mullis, I.V.S., Martin, M.O., Foy, P., & Drucker, K.T. (2012) *PIRLS 2011 international results in reading*. Chestnut Hill, MA: TIMSS & PIRLS International Study Center, Lynch School of Education, Boston College.

Mullis, I.V.S., Martin, M.O., Foy, P., & Arora, A. (2012) *TIMSS 2011 international results in mathematics*. Chestnut Hill, MA: TIMSS & PIRLS International Study Center, Lynch School of Education, Boston College.

Münch, R. (2008) *Globale Eliten, Lokale Autoritäten: Politik unter dem Regime von PISA, McKinsey, & Co*. [Global elites, local authorities: Politics in the regime of PISA and McKinsey & Company]. Frankfurt: Suhrkamp Verlag.

National Center for Education Statistics (2002) *Highlights from the 2000 Program for International Student Assessment of the Program for International Student Assessment (PISA)*. Washington, DC: US Department of Education.

Noah, T. (2012) *The great divergence: America's growing inequality crisis and what we can do about it*. New York: Bloomsbury Press.

OECD (2004) *Learning for tomorrow's world—First results from PISA 2003*. Paris: OECD.

OECD (2007) *Science competencies for tomorrow's world-Executive summary*. Paris: OECD.

OECD (2010) *PISA 2009 results: Executive summary*. Paris: OECD.

OECD (2014) *Country note: Sweden results from TALIS 2013*. Paris: OECD.

OECD (2014) *Country notes, Programme for International Student Assessment (PISA) Results from PISA 2012: United Kingdom*. Paris: OECD.

OECD (2014) *PISA 2012 results in focus: What 15-year-olds know and what they can do with what they know*. Paris: OECD.

OECD (2014) *TALIS 2013 results: An international perspective on teaching and learning*. Paris: OECD.

OECD (2015) *Improving schools in Sweden: An OECD perspective*. Paris: OECD.

Papay, J.P., & Kraft, M.A. (2014) Productivity returns to experience in the teacher labor market: Methodological challenges and new evidence on long-term career improvement. Providence, RI: authors. Retrieved from http://scholar.harvard.edu/files/mkraft/files/jpubec_-_returns_to_experience_manuscript_-_r2.pdf.

Parliament (1988) *Education Reform Act 1988*. London: Her Majesty's Stationery Office. Retrieved from www.legislation.gov.uk/ukpga/1988/40/pdfs/ukpga_19880040_en.pdf.

Rand, A. (1943) *The fountainhead*. Indianapolis, IN: Bobbs Merrill.

Sahlberg, P. (2011) *Finnish lessons: What can the world can learn from educational change in Finland?* New York: Teachers College Press.

Sahlgren, G.H. (2014, July 23) Is Swedish school choice disastrous—Or is the reading of the evidence? Retrieved from www.edchoice.org/is-swedish-school-choice-disastrous-or-is-the-reading-of-the-evidence/.

Sanandaji, T. (2014, July 21) Sweden has an education crisis, but it wasn't caused by school choice. *National Review Online*, p. 3. Retrieved from www.nationalreview.com/agenda/383304/sweden-has-education-crisis-it-wasnt-caused-school-choice-tino-sanandaji?target=author&tid=902932.

Schleicher, A. (2016) *Teaching excellence through professional learning and policy reform: Lessons from around the world*. Paris: OECD.

UNICEF (2013) *Child well-being in rich countries: A comparative overview*. Florence: Innocenti.

Weale, S. (2016, February 26) UK schools suffering as newly qualified teachers "flock abroad." *Guardian*. Retrieved from www.theguardian.com/education/2016/feb/26/uk-schools-suffering-as-new-teachers-flock-abroad-warns-chief-inspector.

Wiborg, S. (2010) *Swedish free schools: Do they work?* London: Centre for Learning and Life Chances in Knowledge Economies and Societies, Institute of Education, University of London.

Zhao, Y. (2014) *Who's afraid of the big bad dragon? Why China has the best (and worst) education system in the world.* San Francisco: Jossey-Bass.

3

THE INTERPRETIVE IMPERATIVE

WE HAVE TO THINK!

In an article entitled "The Worst of Both Worlds: How US and UK Models are Influencing Australian Education," Stephen Dinham of the University of Melbourne has documented how the practices of the " 'Global Educational Reform Movement' (GERM), are finding support and traction in Australia."[1] According to Dinham, under the slogan of increasing school autonomy, Australian schools in some states are becoming detached from democratically-elected local authorities. Teacher education increasingly is disconnected from higher education and research capacity, with for-profit providers moving into new openings for service provision. International publishers that are located in England and the US such as Pearson and McGraw-Hill are among those taking advantage of increased standardized testing and new digital technologies to expand their market share. "Because of Australia's close links with England the USA and their influence," Dinham observes, "it is not surprising that the myths and beliefs underpinning these developments have been accepted almost without evidence or questioning in Australia."[2]

The irony is that Australia has done better than either England or the US on PISA.[3] Australia also does better on many international quality of life indicators, including life expectancy. Australia is not in the position of developing countries that were compelled to adopt No Child Left Behind-like measurements on math and literacy in order to receive education funding from the World Bank. Yet there seems to have been an *imperial imperative* at work that has led even some states in even more successful countries on PISA like Australia to adopt now discredited policies from England and the US.

A century ago, one could have understood such policy borrowing. Australia was part of what was unapologetically called the British Empire. Ever since the London Declaration of 1949, however, Australia has been a free and independent nation. While there still is an emotional attachment to England, England can no more compel Australia to change its education policies than it can any other nation.

For some critics, the OECD is responsible for spreading the key ideas of the GERM. This chapter will show that there is some truth to this charge. But matters are not always so simple. In a study on "The Policy Impact of PISA," Simon Breakspear has shown that "Finland was the most commonly listed influential country/economy" that has been "influential in policy-making processes" in the wake of PISA.[4] Finnish education is the opposite of the GERM.

The impact of the PISA tests in policy formation thus is contradictory, and can best be studied on a case-by-case basis. In this regard Germany is a country that did not follow the *imperial imperative* as some states in Australia are doing and simply implement strategies from abroad. Rather, the country's policy makers adopted a more nuanced *interpretive imperative*. They thought long and hard about what the results indicated. They adopted some reforms piloted in England and the US, but with a lighter touch. They preserved the country's federal structure of education and kept schools under the control of their local democratic authorities. They built up the schools' infrastructure from within rather than launching a frontal assault on them from without. Their reform strategies have made Germany one of the most improved nations on PISA.

So there is a global battle underway for the future of educational change. Some nations, such as the Philippines, Kenya, and Liberia, have followed the US and England with explicit reference to charter schools, academies, and free schools.[5] Some have outsourced public education to for-profit businesses and their philanthropies to secure a competitive advantage in acquiring funding from international organizations that have been beholden to NPM in education, health, and other service sectors. These nations have capitulated to the *imperial imperative*.

Others, however, have evolved their own independent path. These systems have studied evidence, to be sure, but they also have thought about what the numbers say and do not say given their own cultures and values as a nation. These are countries that are showing the way forward. They model a more reflective and sustainable *interpretive imperative*.

Germany is an excellent country to study to learn how the *interpretive imperative* can work. It is one of the few countries that raised its results steadily and rapidly from below to above average in all three academic content areas tested by PISA. Figures 3.1, 3.2, and 3.3 reveal steady German gains in comparison to declining or unchanged results in England, Sweden, and the US.

Germany shows that it is possible to lift a country's schools not in isolated pockets, but as a system. It also shows how a thoughtful, adaptive, and evolutionary ensemble of policies that engages the profession and the public works better than a shock-and-awe approach that relies on perpetual disruption as a policy lever.

I have been studying educational change in Germany for three decades. I read and write German, so I have been able to follow events closely as they have unfolded. Even when similar language is used, German and English speakers can mean different things.

Three examples drawn from a delegation I hosted in Boston illuminate how shared language can carry different meanings in the US and

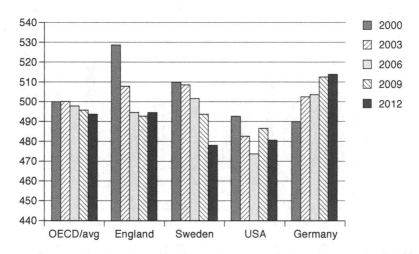

Figure 3.1 PISA Math Scores for the OECD, England, Sweden, the US, and Germany, 2000–2012.

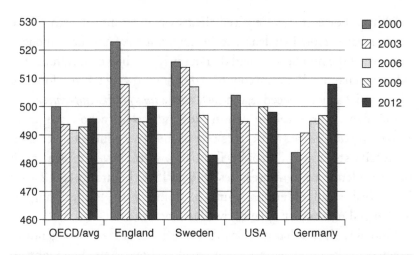

Figure 3.2 PISA Reading Scores for the OECD, England, Sweden, the US, and Germany, 2000–2012 (PISA 2006 results for the US are not available due to sampling errors).

German contexts. First, we visited a charter school and at one point the American educators asked their German counterparts how many of their staff were involved in development. After a moment's confusion, the German principal responded, "All of our staff! Of course, we all are developing our students and ourselves." It took a moment to clarify that in the US context, "development" has come to mean fund-raising. "Development" no longer means the release of human potential.

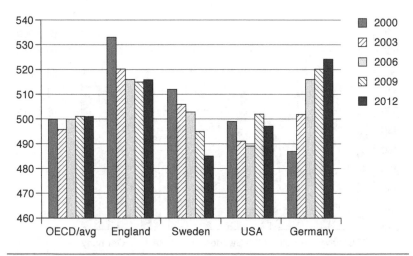

Figure 3.3 PISA Science Scores for the OECD, England, Sweden, the US, and Germany, 2000–2012.

Second, during the same trip, the German delegation was then taken to a "pilot school," which in Boston means a public school that has similarities to charters but has a unionized workforce. As part of the welcome, the US school staff began with a presentation of student achievement on the Massachusetts Comprehensive Assessment System (MCAS). The Germans were confused by this presentation. Did this school not have a unique identity?

For the Germans, educators working in a school had to define the school's own philosophy before any discussion of results could take place. For the US educators, test score results had come to crowd out values. They weren't provided with opportunities to share them in their everyday working environment. "They don't want us to talk about *values*," a principal of another US school told me recently.

The third example, from the same visit by the German educators, refers to what it means to be a teacher in the US and Germany. The members of the German team were all over 40 years old. Their US counterparts were all young, with almost none over 30. The Germans felt empathy for their young US colleagues who had so much to learn. Why were there so few senior staff who could teach their younger colleagues how to pace themselves over time? Where were colleagues who could inform them about the ways that their profession had evolved and how their school had attained its current identity?

To be a teacher in Germany was to become part of a community with a wide age span of individuals. US schools were filled with novices by comparison. Americans were initiating teachers into the profession the hard way, without the benefits of older staff who could help younger ones to develop their teaching repertoires. The young US teachers had few veterans available to help them to learn to pace themselves during the tough stretches so that they would not burn out but rather would stick with the profession for decades to come. This deprived the school of the benefits of the kinds of diversity that come from working with colleagues across generations.

Whether one looks at different understandings of "development," variations in how a school's identity is defined, or what it means to be a teacher from one national setting compared to another, German and US educators experience the profession differently. German educators are not expected to become experts at writing grants to philanthropic organizations; their attention should be focused on teaching and learning. While American policy makers were focused on raising achievement, their German colleagues wanted to achieve broader purposes of education, encompassing moral integrity.

For years Americans were persuaded to accept a reform milieu filled with young social entrepreneurs who threw everything they have at the system for a few years before exiting and moving on to more promising careers. Germans, on the other hand, viewed teaching as a craft requiring consummate skill and not as a temporary stopgap measure before doing something more permanent. These are not minor differences. These are real and substantial contrasts in how education is understood and enacted on a daily basis in the two countries.

Awareness of these differences is important because without this level of understanding the public can be misled into believing that the reason Germany's results have improved is because the country pursued the *imperial imperative* to follow the path established by England, Sweden, and the US. Germany could be misrepresented as the latest country to adopt the NPM model of change. But this is not the case. Germany developed its own reforms that have expanded upon its own educational traditions. These have involved much more attention to building a solid infrastructure and much less reliance on external shocks to the system.

"Strong Performers and Successful Reformers" Revisited

One striking example of how data can be misinterpreted can be found in the chapter on Germany from a widely publicized report entitled *Strong Performers and Successful Reformers in Education: Lessons from PISA for the United States.*[6] This report was accompanied by short video clips available online[7] produced by the Pearson Foundation, the not-for-profit arm of the Pearson Corporation. The purpose of the report and the videos was not merely to report student achievement data, but to recommend strategies that can be replicated by others.

Former US Secretary of Education Arne Duncan commissioned this report. It featured five "high-performing systems": Ontario, Canada;

Shanghai and Hong Kong in China; Finland; Japan; and Singapore.[8] Along with Brazil, Germany was described in a separate chapter as a "rapidly improving" system.[9] The report was intended not only to catalyze reforms in the US but also to "have resonance for a wide range of countries and different types of education systems."[10] In this way it had not only national but also international aspirations. Educators around the world in the most diverse systems were invited to study the report's findings and to apply its recommendations to their schools.

The National Center on the Education and the Economy (NCEE) was authorized to write the report. NCEE Chief Executive Officer and president Marc Tucker and NCEE staff member Betsy Brown Ruzzi wrote the chapter on Germany. Although he criticized some aspects of No Child Left Behind, Tucker has been a leading US advocate for standards-based reform throughout his long and distinguished career. Among many other achievements, he helped to create the National Board on Professional Teaching Standards and the National Skill Standards Board.

Tucker, Ruzzi, and two other NCEE staff members, Susan Sclafani and Jackie Kraemer, led the NCEE team in collaboration with the OECD. Sclafani was Counselor to US Secretary of Education Rod Paige when No Child Left Behind was implemented in the US. She was Vice President of Programs at the Pearson Foundation until the Foundation closed in 2014. The Foundation was required at that time to pay over $7.7 million dollars in fines to New York State for violating guidelines prohibiting philanthropies for supporting the for-profit aspects of their business inappropriately.[11]

None of the lead authors of *Strong Performers and Successful Reformers* actually came from the countries that were held up as exemplars. This contrasts, for example, with the *TIMSS 2011 Encyclopedia*, which was filled with analyses of country policies written by social scientists from the relevant nations.[12] In the TIMSS report, the authors were aware of their country's cultural and historical contexts. They described these objectively, rather than prescribing policies to be developed by others.

In *Strong Performers and Successful Reformers*, few of the authors gave evidence of speaking the languages of the countries that they were describing, unless they were countries in which English was an official language, as was the case with the Canadian province of Ontario and the city-state of Singapore. Not a single German-language document was cited in the entire section on Germany. This lack of familiarity did not, however, prevent the authors from imperiously recommending strategies that others should adopt.

Many of the authors had been leaders in the mainstream reforms of testing and standardization in the US over decades. Their findings aligned with their long-standing commitments and beliefs. According to the authors, "Virtually every country featured in this volume also mirror [sic] Race to the Top's effort to support the recruitment, development, rewarding and retaining of effective teachers and principals."[13] Yet "Race to the Top" came years after the policies in Canada, Singapore, and Finland to secure teacher quality had been put in place, and its own policy strategy bears no resemblance to them. None of those jurisdictions have ever supported end-runs on teacher professionalism like Teach for America that place novices in front of their students in challenging urban schools. The US is anything but a leader in teacher quality. The report's authors misinterpreted the policies of improving systems they have failed to learn from.

The imperial attitude that characterizes *Strong Performers and Successful Reformers* is evident throughout the country chapter on Germany. Germany is famous for having one of the world's most rigorous teacher education policies. To become a teacher in Germany requires a minimum of five-and-a-half years of training, "the longest pre-service teacher training among PISA 2012 countries."[14] This extensive training has real and tangible benefits. German teachers must have the equivalent of two US master's degrees as well as extensive practicum experience. Professional ethics and responsibilities are taken seriously. The public in turn supports educators. The salaries of German teachers are among the best in the world.

Yet when Tucker and Ruzzi select a quote on the outstanding German teacher education system, they do not reference any of the thousands of professionals who have given that system its high quality. Instead, they cite the Director of "Teach First Germany," the German equivalent of Teach for America. They do not let their readers know that "Teach First" in Germany, unlike Teach for America, is only able to place its graduates in schools as teachers' aides, not as classroom teachers who are accountable for the students' learning. This is a striking contrast with the US experience, where Teach for America graduates are thrown with full responsibility into some of the nation's most difficult and poorly resourced classrooms, with barely six weeks of summertime preparation. Typically, "Teach First" graduates in Germany are assigned to work with small groups of students who need extra assistance, not whole classes. "Teach First" in Germany has not prepared a *single* classroom teacher—only teachers' aides.

To be blunt, American educators are less well prepared than German teachers. They generally enter the profession with only the equivalent of a bachelor's degree. American teachers are expected to implement new reforms so their students can be tested with fidelity. They are not encouraged to exercise the continual intellectual reflection and ongoing adjustments that are at the heart of the teaching profession in Germany. While US educators do have some job security, this has been undercut in recent years. By comparison, all German teachers enjoy high status as civil servants, a part of a government that has a sterling reputation for incorruptibility.

This respect for the teaching profession has meant that post-PISA reforms in Germany have had less of a managerial tone than those in the US. Although it is true that there is more testing in Germany today than before the first PISA results were released, this is almost always done by following the Finnish model of testing a sample of subpopulations of students rather than a census of all of them. There has been no German analogue to the high stakes testing of all students in grades 3–8 that followed the passage of No Child Left Behind in the US. This has sheltered German educators from the curriculum narrowing that occurred in US schools.

German students are taught to respect the rigorous demands that accompany teaching and learning, along with a long intellectual lineage of education that dates back to the German Enlightenment as the venue for one's self-realization. This has made it practically impossible in Germany to introduce the kinds of public ranking of teachers and schools that have appeared in US media outlets. Given this public reluctance to identify struggling teachers and schools, there also is no reliance on the threat of school closures and staff dismissals to catalyze school improvement.

In the German context, US-style reforms that hold up individuals for public humiliation evoke memories of the Nazi past and the communist regime of former East Germany. These forms of government violated the individual's right to privacy, and even denied that individuals had such rights. Since the Berlin Wall only came down in 1989, there are many Germans today for whom the sinister aspects of state surveillance are a living memory.

To Germans, if teachers are failing to improve student learning, or principals are not lifting results in their schools, these matters should be handled with respect for the dignity and integrity of the individuals involved. Research from the US has shown for decades that measures of teacher effectiveness are unstable over time.[15] Teachers have good and bad years. A single misbehaving student can wreak havoc on the best-laid lesson plans. Districts introduce new curricula that often produce a dip in results in the early stages of adaptation. These are well-known professional challenges. There are other ways to improve education than placing such a focus on testing, rewards, and sanctions—especially since the individuals who are most likely to be stigmatized by low student test score results generally are those who have volunteered to teach in poor, working-class, or immigrant communities.

In Germany no public revenues go into pay-for-performance schemes that get educators focused on pumping up test scores rather than addressing the broader purposes of education. Instead, German education is rooted in an intellectual and educational tradition anchored in the philosophy of the German Enlightenment from Immanuel Kant to Georg Wilhelm Friedrich Hegel.[16] Education is not viewed as an assembly-line function but as an evolutionary process that advances from one stage of life to another, guided by a sympathetic teacher and other supportive adults.

This humanistic orientation is reflected in the German attitude toward school choice. There are numerous kinds of schools that students can select from, especially among secondary schools in larger cities, and in this way German education has parallels to schooling in most other systems. In some instances, when industry leaders are especially invested in preparing certain kinds of workers, the vocational schools are better resourced than the classical *Gymnasia* that prepare students for universities. Since the same word is used in

Germany to designate one as a "professional" whether one works with one's hands or with one's mind (*Beruf*, or a "calling"), there is equivalence among different occupations in their nomenclature.

These contextual factors give school choice a different meaning than it occupies in other reform discourses. It is one's actual skills as an electrician, machinist, or carpenter that matter if you are in a vocational school, not your test scores. This Germanic approach to choice is accompanied by different kinds of assessments. It also means that the ideological skirmishes that have marked US or English debates among advocates or critics of charter schools or academies have no parallel in Germany.

Germany did not pursue policies similar to those developed by England, Sweden, and the US. A number of Germany's policies have greater affinities with the Finnish model of social solidarity, disciplinary integrity, and assessment through demonstrations in the vocational education sector. Germany has had the courage to study its own system, to acknowledge its inadequacies, and to persevere with reforms fitted to its own preferred future.

None of this has been easy and there have been ferocious debates every step of the way. In Germany there is no clear explanation of how PISA results have improved, and there are plenty of arguments about what the rise in results means. Skeptics point to chance or dumb luck rather than any deliberate strategy. For example, the percentage of students attending the *Gymnasia* with their more academically demanding curricula has been rising steadily in recent decades and pre-dates PISA. This population shift to a more academically demanding curriculum likely has contributed to improved PISA results. However, with less than a third of German students attending *Gymnasia*, other factors must be influential.

What are those factors?

In Simon Breakspear's 2012 report on "The Policy Impact of PISA," Germany is identified as a nation with an "intense" level of responsiveness to the assessment. Germany's response to what was called "PISA shock" has not simply been limited to government actions.[17] In free and pluralistic societies it is important to investigate arenas that lie beyond government control that also make contributions to educational change. Germany is famous for its densely textured voluntary associations that play important roles in advancing social progress. Let's turn to two of these next.

Civil Society Organizations Initiate and Sustain Change

Reports that focus on the technical and policy-specific dimensions of educational change overlook the role that civil society associations and professional organizations play in improving education. It is as if the only serious change agent could ever be the government or that the only real catalyst for change could be data. There is no room for changes that could come from a unified profession or an organized public.

This absence is partially understandable because so many transnational organizations like the OECD and the World Bank rely on government contracts to fund their work. Emphasizing the state's role in creating policies that produce change is appealing to policy makers because they need to be re-elected. In many cases, however, it exaggerates the government's role in influencing results.

Change actually comes from many different sectors. For example, the Freedom Schools of the Civil Rights Movement in the US were not organized by the government but in spite of it.[18] Recent protests by students in Chile for greater equity in education began as spontaneous eruptions of discontent and then brought teachers' unions and other syndicates into their fold before electing a new generation of leaders to the country's parliament.[19] In the US, protests by teacher unions against standardized testing and the citizen-driven opt-out movement toppled the No Child Left Behind Act. Governments can and do play positive roles in education, but sometimes they have to be challenged, circumvented, or overcome to promote higher levels of learning or more equitable experiences of education for all students.

In Germany, civil society and professional associations have been uplifting education and its results, including PISA, for many years. These groups are independent of government and are omitted from *Strong Performers and Successful Reformers*. Their leadership and efficacy needs to be incorporated into any analysis of Germany's rising PISA results.

The German School Academy

One group that has shown leadership is the German School Academy, an initiative supported by the Robert Bosch and Heidehof Foundations since 2007. The foundations "sought to take on nothing less than to connect the public discussions that had begun with the PISA studies to positive examples of schools and instruction."[20] The foundations connected their work with a previous initiative of one of Germany's largest newsweeklies, the *Stern*, and with ZDF, one of Germany's major television channels, so that its activities would be broadcast across the country.

Until 2015, the Academy was known as the "Academy of the German School Prize" and it focused on six criteria to select awards for schools. These are described in what follows next. It is important to attend to subtleties in how the particular philosophy of the Academy has been enacted. Similarities in translated terms should not be viewed as identical with current usage in nations in which the old imperatives have become institutionalized.

The first of these six criteria is *achievement*. This entails not just high results in the core subjects of math, foreign languages, and science. It also encompasses the arts, sports, and interdisciplinary projects. Achievement can mean making a documentary film, launching a new app, or preserving a historical or cultural artifact in the community. At the Kleine Kielstrasse Elementary School in Dortmund, the first task of the principal was to talk with prostitutes and drug dealers at a nearby intersection to secure their cooperation in moving off the streets when students were coming to school in the morning or leaving in the afternoon. The second step was to get immigrant parents involved in the schools; this was done by setting up a room with sewing machines where mothers could come and work with one another in an atmosphere of relaxed conviviality. Finally, the principal worked with the teachers to produce evidence of student learning not on standardized tests, but on innovative portfolios that tracked student learning over time.

The second criterion is the school's engagement with *diversity*. This includes learning disabilities, students' socio-economic backgrounds, and the students' ethnic and linguistic heritages. Given Germany's troubled past with diversity, establishing this criterion aligns with the nation's efforts to face up to the darker chapters of its history, to learn from them, and to chart a more tolerant future. At the Robert Bosch Comprehensive School in Hildesheim, part of its award for diversity entailed taking care of a Jewish cemetery near the school and establishing contact with Holocaust survivors from their community. Students from the school escorted me to the cemetery and described their efforts to maintain it as part of their civic responsibility.

The third criterion is *pedagogy*. The selection committee looks for "schools that are engaged to ensure that students take responsibility for their own learning" and "facilitate the integration of learning sites outside of the school."[21] In Germany, pedagogy does not refer to the teachers' ability to deliver content alone. This would violate the profession's emphasis on establishing an optimal learning climate in which all students can thrive. This tradition has worked out theories of "general didactics" that are taught to all student teachers in Germany. ("Didactics" here is a false cognate; it means the opposite of lecturing, as the term is understood in English.) "General didactics" in Germany emphasizes the importance of educating the whole child in her or his moral, intellectual, and physical totality.[22] The didactic tradition requires that student learning is not encapsulated by an inward-looking school but instead is open to the world.

The fourth criterion of the selection committee is *responsibility* in how schools promote "respectful engagement with one another, creative possibilities for nonviolent conflict resolution, and careful interactions with things that are not only postulated but actually brought to practical fruition."[23] A good school develops learners who are polite and accept disagreement as inevitable and even desirable in an open and free society. These are socio-emotional and democratic foundations of a good education.

The fifth criterion relates to *school climate*. The school is assessed on its ability to establish an atmosphere in which "students, teachers, and parents like to go to the school; in which pedagogically fruitful relationships are established with persons outside of the school and address the public at large."[24] A good school cannot produce high learning outcomes for the public if this results in private misery for the students.

The sixth criterion is the *school as a learning institution* in which educators work together in a way that is "independent and sustainable."[25] Educators visit one another's classrooms, provide each other with feedback, and visit other schools in order to acquire new ideas. They attend conferences hosted by the Academy to hear guest speakers and to share their innovations with one another. These are especially important for educators teaching in schools characterized by high rates of inter-generational poverty in northern cities such as Hamburg, Essen, and Bremerhaven.

When the Academy of the German School Prize gave its first award in Berlin, the President of the Federal Republic, Horst Köhler,[26] gave the welcoming address with the title, "It Also Can Work Another Way." While only a small percentage of the roughly 44,000 German schools apply for the award, its high-level visibility, its emphasis on diverse forms of experimentation, and its humanistic thrust has made it a powerful influence in the German educational landscape. Schools that focus on immigrant youth, create novel forms of blended instruction for students with and without disabilities, and generate unique pedagogical concepts organized around the environment, the arts, or the sciences have won the award.

In 2015 the Academy of the German School Prize reorganized its activities to de-emphasize the competitive nature of the award and was given a new name: the German School Academy. The German School Academy provides educators with holistic criteria with which to assess, deepen, and disseminate their work. It is working with the television company ARD to promote the Academy (rather than the original television company known as ZDF), so that the public is informed about promising educational developments. The schools affiliated with the Academy have played important roles in disseminating diverse reform models, such as the teacher evaluation protocols developed at the Robert Bosch Comprehensive School, throughout the country.[27] These have contributed to the higher rate of teacher collaboration around lesson planning that exists in Germany than is the average for OECD nations.[28]

One Square Kilometer of Education

When the Berlin Wall came down in 1989, Berlin rapidly transformed itself from a divided city into an international hot spot for artists and entrepreneurs. Cheap flats in East Berlin were snatched up at lightning speed, trendy new clubs opened in nooks and crannies all over the city, and real estate prices surged. It suddenly became effortless to stroll from the elegant Café Einstein on the Kürfurstenstrasse to the spectacular Museum Island without having to wait to get through passport control. Only the smell of East Berlin's antiquated sewage system served as a rancid reminder of the drab communist past in an otherwise transformed city.

Beyond the glitter, however, another Berlin persisted, and nowhere more than in gritty Neukölln, a neighborhood with half of its population on welfare and a 40 percent jobless rate in the first decade of the new millennium. Schools in Neukölln were populated with over 80 percent immigrant youth, almost all from the Middle East, and almost all of whom had German as a second language. Less than 1 percent of all of the city's teachers had immigrant backgrounds, leaving few adults to serve as role models or translators with personal experience of the challenges in adapting to the dominant culture. The immigrant youth typically found themselves tracked to the lowest level of Germany's secondary schools (the *Hauptschule*). Many of their teachers had been prepared in former communist East Germany. This walled-off country was so closed to outsiders that in the 1980s its residents were forbidden to travel even to neighboring Soviet satellites for fear of ideological contamination.

Such social settings are ripe for all kinds of cross-cultural miscommunication and conflict. In Neukölln all of the social pressures broke into the open in February 2006 when Petra Eggebrecht, principal of the Rütli School, authored a letter to the Berlin Senate that was leaked to the press. Eggebrecht described a school that had come to a dead end in which students constantly defied their teachers, resisted any form of instruction, and committed random acts of violence. Parents did not respond to phone calls and educators felt abandoned by the community. Eggebrecht called for immediate assistance from a crisis intervention team and for the school's abolition as an outmoded *Hauptschule* into something more inclusive and aspirational.

The fact that Eggebrecht's letter found its way to the press was a public relations nightmare for the school system. Reporters flocked to the Rütli School. Some politicians made statements that inflamed social resentments of immigrants. The previous principal of the school was interviewed by the press and blamed the problems of the school on insufficient faculty and teachers who were unprepared to educate culturally diverse students.

"The Rütli School became a symbol of a system that didn't possess the strength to educate its weakest students," the *Berliner Zeitung* later reported.[29] If any school in Germany had reached the pedagogical equivalent of Ground Zero, it was the Rütli Schule.

Ten years later, however, the school has been transformed. The old *Hauptschule* that prepared students only for blue-collar jobs was abolished in the 2008–2009 school year. Cordula Heckmann was appointed as the school's new principal in 2009, and the Rütli School began to offer college preparatory classes. Students now document their own learning through portfolios that allow them to reflect on their development and to present it persuasively to others. In 2014 the Rütli School graduated its first class with the *Abitur* that will allow them to enter university studies. Eighteen of the 23 students with the *Abitur* were of immigrant backgrounds. The student dropout rate plummeted from over 20 percent in 2006 to between 5 and 6 percent in 2014. One indication of the rebirth of the Rütli School is that other schools in Neukölln are clamoring for a similar infusion of new resources—perhaps the ultimate testimony to its success.

Positive changes are evident not just in the building but also in the environment of the school. How could one capitalize upon all of the assets that reside in an immigrant community and bring them into better coordination with one another to support the children who attend the Rütli School? "Campus Rütli," a network of resources near the school, now brings sparkle to Neukölln. Early childhood centers, job training facilities, other public schools, and a new art gallery are all networked into Campus Rütli. An after-school program fostering the arts provides visitors with a creativity-rich introduction to Campus Rütli. Teachers work collaboratively to establish long-term goals, instruction is individualized, and non-profits, philanthropies, and government agencies support the community.

Beyond these important incremental changes, the Rütli School engaged the city government of Berlin and some of Germany's most creative foundations in developing a new concept, "One Square Kilometer of Education," to respond not only to the crisis at the Rütli School but the need for Germany to better welcome its surging numbers of immigrants. This bears many similarities with the Harlem's Children Zone in New York City but also a decisive difference: "One Square Kilometer of Education" is working with traditional public schools, not charter schools that stand outside of the larger system.

I have served as technical advisor on the "One Square Kilometer of Education" project over the past ten years. What began as an almost desperate shot-in-the-dark project to revive a crisis-ridden school has evolved into a firmly embedded network of community and educational supports for the Rütli School. The school hosts visitors from throughout Germany on a regular basis. Furthermore, the pioneering work of "One Square Kilometer of Education" was prescient. Given the hundreds of thousands of new immigrants arriving in Germany in the wake of the Syrian conflict, "One Square Kilometer of Education" offers a promising model of achievement with integrity that can be an inspiration for all.

The Cultural Ministers' Conference

The German School Academy and the "One Square Kilometer of Education" project are bottom-up civil society initiatives to improve German schools and society. Such undertakings are often left out of mainstream policy discourse. For some it is government policy, and government policy alone, that is responsible for student learning in the end.

But for educational change to be sustainable it must engage those closest to the students—especially classroom teachers and school administrators—with policy makers and researchers in communities of inquiry. Educators need opportunities to be involved in the shaping of policies since they will be the ones whose actions will determine whether the policies are successful or not in the long run.

We shouldn't be surprised to learn that there is reluctance among Germans to invest too much authority in the central government. When Nazi Germany was defeated at the end of World War II, the Allies, led by the US, insisted on creating a federal system of education to prevent the abuses of government that had occurred under the Third Reich.[30] But this federal system originally brought mixed blessings. Top-down authoritarian control had been avoided, but system coherence and consistency were also weak. Even before the first PISA results were published, Germans were confronted with other assessment data from TIMSS in 1996 indicating that their students' skills were widely divergent not only across but also within states.[31] When PISA results were released Germans learned that the comparison of students' math results from the worst performing states revealed that they were two years behind the top performers. Further analysis showed that math teachers focused excessively on the technical nature of math and gave inadequate attention to problem solving and complex modeling. Since PISA aspires to measure real-world skills, these curricular imbalances were reflected in item analyses of students' results.

To address these discrepancies, Germans have agreed upon learning standards for the whole country. But this has been done differently from elsewhere. The standards have not entailed testing all students in grades 3–8 to establish adequate yearly progress. Nor have they been used to benchmark teachers' salary bonuses to their students' test scores. The intention has been *educational*—to gather information to improve *learning*.

After the first PISA results were released in Germany, the Cultural Ministers' Conference (*Kultusministerkonferenz* or KMK) representing all 16 federal states, commissioned researchers to recommend national standards in collaboration with teachers. The standards were correlated with educational goals, competency models, and assessments. In these ways greater coherence was sponsored throughout the school system, although in almost every other way each state still places its unique policy imprimatur on its schools. Secondary school standards in mathematics were approved in 2003 and primary school standards were approved in 2004.

Since standards by themselves do nothing to improve teaching and learning, the KMK also established networks of researchers and practitioners to work with classroom teachers and principals to improve instruction, curricula, and assessments. A new Institute for Improvement of Educational Quality was established at Humboldt University in Berlin. Its task is to monitor student achievement results, to provide supportive materials for educators, and to develop new assessments.

All students in Germany are now tested in either German or mathematics at grades 3 and 8. Each state is free to determine which subject it will assess in a given year and at which grade level. The endeavor is to establish greater clarity across the country for what students should know and be able to do. This is transparency with a light touch.

As was the case with the Academy of the German School Prize and "One Square Kilometer of Education," it is not possible to prove that the creation of national standards or networks of educators have caused Germany's improving PISA results. Even if they did, Germany preceded the US in this regard, so its successes cannot have been derived from US experience.

Educational change is shaped by the interaction of government policy, professional reforms, and civil society initiatives. We can't just look at top-down policies, appeal to strategies that have been imperially transferred from systems elsewhere, or even assume that all real change percolates from the bottom up. Taking Germany as an example, we have learned that educational change is more complicated than any of that. Change is about the interactions of many parts of complex systems that span all of the way from government policies through civil society straight into the nexus of teaching and learning that occurs at the classroom level. Getting all of those parts to work together is what makes it so challenging.

Conclusion

Germany is a peaceful, multicultural democracy that avoids touting its own merits, although others increasingly are doing so. In 2013 French public intellectual Alain Minc published *Vive l'Allegmagne!* (*Long Live Germany!*), praising Germany's successful reinvention as the continent's foremost multicultural democracy.[32] In 2014 Italian political scientist Angelo Bolaffi published *Curo Tedesco* (*German Heart*), arguing that Europeans today should rally behind Germany's steadfast dedication to human rights and social democracy.[33] Significantly, Minc and Bolaffi are both of Jewish descent. They don't confuse Germany's past with its efforts to lead Europe and the world toward a better and more inclusive future.

For historical reasons, we should not expect Germans to promote their improving educational system through inspirational speeches or commentaries. No one is promoting "German Lessons" for others to learn from. Circumspection about national pride has become a German character trait. Elsewhere, other nations have been all too eager to adopt practices from powerful nations even when they have stalled in their home countries. This chapter has shown us that we can do better.

The first new imperative of educational change concerned the need to get past *ideologies* to study *evidence* of learning and how that is related to government policies. The second imperative described in the current chapter indicates that one highly impactful report, the OECD's *Strong Performers and Successful Reformers*, with its *imperial* pretentions must be viewed critically. We must become better at *interpreting* the change for ourselves so that it fits our own traditions and maximizes our own potential.

Who should lead this *interpretive imperative*? Ideally, those at the vanguard of this movement should be educators themselves, spanning the spectrum of the whole, united profession from classroom teachers to principals to superintendents. Ironically, however, these very same individuals have been most disempowered by the old imperatives. Two-thirds of teachers surveyed on the TALIS study report that their schools are hostile to innovations. Only one-third communicate that teaching is respected in their country. Four-fifths indicate that when they are evaluated this is done for managerial reasons and not to improve teaching and learning. The problems teachers face are not due to their teacher education programs, because overwhelming majorities report that these did a good job preparing them for the classroom. The problem has to do with constraints they face once they enter the classroom. These teachers are struggling under an increasingly anachronistic *prescriptive imperative*.

Teachers want to get beyond this state of affairs. They want to be able to develop creative lesson plans, to work on teams, and to make good judgments. They want to show what they can do and to be proud members of a guild that helps them to go on improving throughout their careers. But they will never get there with an atomistic approach to change that gives them a tick in one box for writing a behavioral objective on the blackboard and another tick for reviewing the main ideas at the end of a lesson, important as such practices might be. They will rather need an entirely new recasting of their work. This is at the heart of the new *professional imperative*.

Notes

1 Dinham, S. (2015) The worst of both worlds: How US and UK models are influencing Australian education. *Education Policy Analysis Archives* 23(49), 1–15.
2 Dinham, The worst of both worlds, p. 12.
3 OECD (2013) *PISA 2012 results in focus: What 15-year-olds know and what they do with what they know*. Paris: OECD.
4 Breakspear, S. (2012) *The policy impact of PISA: An exploration of the normative effects of international benchmarking in school system performance*. Paris: OECD, p. 17.
5 See Verger, A., Lubienski, C., & Steiner-Khamsi, G. (2016) *World yearbook of education 2016: The global education industry*. New York: Routledge, and Adamson, A., Astrand, B., & Darling-Hammond, L. (Eds.) (2016) *Global education reform: How privatization and public investment influence education outcomes*. New York: Routledge.
6 OECD (2010) *Strong performers and successful reformers: Lesson from PISA for the United States*. Paris: OECD.
7 To view the videos go to www.pearsonfoundation.org/oecd.
8 OECD, *Strong performers and successful reformers*, p. 16.
9 OECD, *Strong performers and successful reformers*, p. 16.
10 OECD, *Strong performers and successful reformers*, p. 9.
11 Strauss, V. (2014, November 19) Pearson Foundation closing (after paying big fines for helping corporate parent). *Washington Post*. Retrieved from www.washingtonpost.com/news/answer-sheet/wp/2014/11/19/pearson-foundation-closing-after-paying-big-fines-for-helping-corporate-parent/.
12 Mullis, I.V.S., Martin, M.O., Minnich, C.A., Stanco, G.M., Arora, A., Centurino, V.A.S., & Castle, C.E. (2012) *TIMSS 2011 encyclopedia: Education policy and curriculum in mathematics and science*. TIMSS & PIRLS International Study Center, Lynch School of Education, Boston College.
13 OECD, *Strong performers and successful reformers*, p. 230.
14 OECD (2014) *Education policy outlook: Germany*. Paris: OECD, p. 10.
15 Braun, H.I. (2005) *Using student progress to evaluate teachers: A primer on value-added models*. Princeton, NJ: Educational Testing Service.
16 See Shirley, D. (2008) The coming of post-standardization in education: What role for the German *Didaktik* tradition? *Zeitschrift für Erziehungswissenschaft Sonderheft* 10(9), 35–46, and Shirley, D. (2009) American perspectives on German educational theory and research—A closer look at both the American educational context and the German *Didaktik* tradition. In: Arnold, K.H., Blömeke, S.,

Messner, R., & Schlömerkemper, J. (Eds.) *Allgemeine Didaktik und Lehr-Lernforschung: Kontroversen und Entwicklungsperspektiven einer Wissenschaft vom Unterricht.* Bad Heilbrunn: Verlag Julius Klinkhardt, pp. 195–210.

17 Breakspear, *The policy impact of PISA*, p. 5.

18 Payne, C. (1995) *I've got the light of freedom: The organizing tradition and the Mississippi freedom struggle.* Berkeley: University of California Press.

19 Castro-Hidalgo, A., & Gómez-Álvarez, L. (2016) Chile: A long-term neoliberal experiment and its impact on the quality and equity of education. In: Adamson et al., *Global education reform*, pp. 16–49.

20 Hamm, I., & Madelung, E. (2007) Vorwort. In Fauser, P., Prenzel, M., & Schratz, M. (Eds.) *Was für Schulen! Gute Schule in Deutschland* [What schools! The good school in Germany]. Seelze-Velber: Klett, p. 1.

21 Schratz, M., Pant, H.A., & Wischer, B. (2014) *Was für Schulen! Leistung sichtbar machen—Beispiele guter Praxis* [What schools! Make achievement visible—Examples of good practice]. Seelze: Klett/Kallmeyer, p. 13.

22 Westbury, I., Hopmann, S., & Riquarts, K. (2000) *Teaching as a reflective practice: The German Didaktik tradition.* Mahwah, NJ: Lawrence Erlbaum.

23 Schratz et al., *Was für Schulen!*, p. 13.

24 Schratz et al., *Was für Schulen!*, p. 13.

25 Schratz et al., *Was für Schulen!*, p. 13.

26 Köhler, H. (2006) Es geht auch anders! [It works another way!] In Fauser, P., Prenzel, M., & Schratz, M. (Eds.) *Was für Schulen! Gute Schule in Deutschland* [What schools! The good school in Germany]. Seelze-Velber: Klett Fauser, p. 4.

27 Otto, J., & Spiewak, M. (2016, February 25) Nie mehr allein [Never again alone]. *Die Zeit*, p. 62.

28 Richter, D., & Pant, H.A. (2016) *Lehrerkooperation in Deutschland* [Teacher cooperation in Germany]. Gütersloh, Germany: Bertelsmann Foundation.

29 Klesmann, M. (2014) Erste Abiturienten an der Rütlischule [First graduates from the Rütlischule]. *Berliner Zeitung.* Retrieved from www.berliner-zeitung. de/berlin/gemeinschaftsschule-ruetli-erste-abiturienten-an-der-ruetli-schule, 10809148,27675096.html.

30 Tent, J.F. (1982) *Mission on the Rhine: Reeducation and denazification in America-occupied Germany.* Chicago: University of Chicago Press.

31 Beaton, A., Mullis, I.V.S., Martin, M.O., Gonzalez, E.J., Kelly, D.L., & Smith, T.A. (1996) *Mathematics achievement in the middle school years: The IEA's Third International Mathematics and Science Study (TIMSS).* Chestnut Hill, MA: TIMSS & PIRLS International Study Center, Lynch School of Education, Boston College.

32 Minc, A. (2013) *Vive l'Allegmagne!* [Long live Germany!]. Paris: Grasset.

33 Bolaffi, A. (2014) *Cuore Tedesco: Il modello Germania, l'Italia e la crisi europea* [German heart: The German model, Italy, and the European crisis]. Rome: Donzelli.

References

Adamson, F., Åstrand, B., & Darling-Hammond, L. (Eds.) (2016) *Global education reform: How privatization and public investment influence education outcomes.* New York: Routledge.

Beaton, A., Mullis, I.V.S., Martin, M.O., Gonzalez, E.J., Kelly, D.L., & Smith, T.A. (1996) *Mathematics achievement in the middle school years: The IEA's Third International Mathematics and Science Study (TIMSS).* Chestnut Hill, MA: TIMSS & PIRLS International Study Center, Lynch School of Education, Boston College.

Bolaffi, A. (2014) *Cuore Tedesco: Il modello Germania, l'Italia e la crisi europea* [German heart: The German model, Italy, and the European crisis]. Rome: Donzelli.

Braun, H.I. (2005) *Using student progress to evaluate teachers: A primer on value-added models.* Princeton, NJ: Educational Testing Service.

Breakspear, S. (2012) *The policy impact of PISA: An exploration of the normative effects of international benchmarking in school system performance.* Paris: OECD.

Castro-Hidalgo, A., & Gómez-Álvarez, L. (2016) Chile: A long-term neo-liberal experiment and its impact on the quality and equity of education. In: Adamson, A., Astrand, B., & Darling-Hammond, L. (Eds.) *Global education reform: How privatization and public investment influence education outcomes.* New York: Routledge, pp. 16–49.

Dinham, S. (2015) The worst of both worlds: How US and UK models are influencing Australian education. *Education Policy Analysis Archives* 23(49), 1–15.

Hamm, I., & Madelung, E. (2007) Vorwort. In Fauser, P., Prenzel, M., & Schratz, M. (Eds.) *Was für Schulen! Gute Schule in Deutschland* [What schools! The good school in Germany]. Seelze-Velber: Klett.

Klesmann, M. (2014) Erste Abiturienten an der Rütlischule [First graduates from the Rütlischule]. *Berliner Zeitung.* Retrieved from www.berliner-zeitung.de/berlin/gemeinschaftsschule-ruetli-erste-abiturienten-an-der-ruetli-schule,10809148,27675096.html.

Köhler, H. (2006) Es geht auch anders! [It works another way!] In Fauser, P., Prenzel, M., & Schratz, M. (Eds.) *Was für Schulen! Gute Schule in Deutschland* [What schools! The good school in Germany]. Seelze-Velber: Klett, p. 4.

Minc, A. (2013) *Vive l'Allegmagne!* [Long live Germany!]. Paris: Grasset.

Mullis, I.V.S., Martin, M.O., Minnich, C.A., Stanco, G.M., Arora, A., Centurino, V.A.S., & Castle, C.E. (2012) *TIMSS 2011 encyclopedia: Education policy and curriculum in mathematics and science.* TIMSS & PIRLS International Study Center, Lynch School of Education, Boston College.

OECD (2010) *Strong performers and successful reformers: Lessons from PISA for the United States.* Paris: OECD.

OECD (2013) *PISA 2012 results in focus: What 15-year-olds know and what they do with what they know.* Paris: OECD.

OECD (2014) *Education policy outlook: Germany.* Paris: OECD.

Otto, J., & Spiewak, M. (2016, February 25) Nie mehr allein [Never again alone]. *Die Zeit,* p. 62.

Payne, C. (1995) *I've got the light of freedom: The organizing tradition and the Mississippi freedom struggle.* Berkeley: University of California Press.

Richter, D., & Pant, H.A. (2016) *Lehrerkooperation in Deutschland* [Teacher cooperation in Germany]. Gütersloh, Germany: Bertelsmann Foundation.

Schratz, M., Pant, H.A., & Wischer, B. (2014) *Was für Schulen! Leistung sichtbar machen—Beispiele guter Praxis* [What schools! Make achievement visible—Examples of good practice]. Seelze: Klett/Kallmeyer.

Shirley, D. (2008) The coming of post-standardization in education: What role for the German *Didaktik* tradition? *Zeitschrift für Erziehungswissenschaft Sonderheft* 10(9), 35–46.

Shirley, D. (2009) American perspectives on German educational theory and research—A closer look at both the American educational context and the German *Didaktik* tradition. In: Arnold, K.H., Blömeke, S., Messner, R., & Schlömerkemper, J. (Eds.) *Allgemeine Didaktik und Lehr-Lernforschung: Kontroversen und Entwicklungsperspektiven einer Wissenschaft vom Unterricht.* Bad Heilbrunn: Verlag Julius Klinkhardt, pp. 195–210.

Strauss, V. (2014, November 19) Pearson Foundation closing (after paying big fines for helping corporate parent). *Washington Post.* Retrieved from www.washingtonpost.com/news/answer-sheet/wp/2014/11/19/pearson-foundation-closing-after-paying-big-fines-for-helping-corporate-parent/.

Tent, J.F. (1982) *Mission on the Rhine: Reeducation and denazification in American-occupied Germany.* Chicago: University of Chicago Press.

Verger, A., Lubienski, C., & Steiner-Khamsi, G. (2016) *World yearbook of education 2016: The global education industry.* New York: Routledge.

Westbury, I., Hopmann, S., & Riquarts, K. (2000) *Teaching as a reflective practice: The German Didaktik tradition.* Mahwah, NJ: Lawrence Erlbaum.

4

THE PROFESSIONAL IMPERATIVE

NEW FRAMEWORKS FOR CHANGE

In an affluent district on the east coast of the US, elementary school teachers spend every day in the month before state tests are administered giving their students multiple-choice items to review for the English language components. In an urban high school in Arizona, an economics teacher is required to begin the school year by giving students a pre-test that will be compared with a post-test at the end of the year. In a rural school district in the Pacific Northwest, teachers cut back on fiction so that their curriculum is better aligned with the Common Core State Standards.

Such practices are slowly but surely draining the magic out of education. Too many US students today are reading mainly informational text, so they will know how to comprehend manuals in order to compete successfully with China and India. One impatient student who was bored with informational text asked me, "Why can't we ever read something interesting in this school?" When I asked him what he had in mind, his response was, "Something exciting, like something about dragons!" This student pulled on my heartstrings because like many others, I was an indifferent reader until I stumbled upon J.R.R. Tolkien when I was in junior high school. The madcap escapades of the hobbits were a revelation to me. To be whisked away from the awkwardness of early adolescence into the fabulous fantasy of Middle Earth was the ultimate liberation for my restless mind.

Teachers who are sympathetic to their students' cravings to be carried far away from their humdrum lives have had a tough time under the old imperatives. I recently observed an English class of

10th graders in the US where the students were just starting their first novel of the year—*in February*. By contrast, when I was in high school decades ago, by this point of time our English teachers were throwing all kinds of demanding classical and contemporary authors at us—so we would grapple with issues like death, madness, and prejudice. What are too many students today getting instead? They are reading informational text.

An old *prescriptive imperative* from government at the federal, state, and district levels undermined teachers' best judgments about pedagogy, curriculum, and assessment. This is not just a problem in the US. Roughly one-third of teachers in the most recent TALIS survey indicated that they do not select the curricula that they teach and one in five does not choose the assessments.[1] In practice, what this means is that teachers in many systems are provided with a scripted curriculum to follow in preparing students for tests that they have not designed. In some cases, teachers find themselves receiving instructional coaching from the sales agents of the companies that provide the curriculum or that designed the tests.[2]

In *The Mindful Teacher*, my co-author Elizabeth MacDonald and I describe such phenomena as "alienated teaching."[3] This is what happens when teachers adjust their pedagogies and their curricula out of a sense of respect for and obligation to higher authorities, even when the teachers know they are eroding their professional judgment. Research by Corrie Stone-Johnson[4] has documented that once alienated teaching becomes pervasive in a school it impacts everyone, even school counselors, who just like teachers, are pressed into bureaucratic compliance.

If anything can be learned from the No Child Left Behind Act in the US, it is that excessive government intervention in schools doesn't work. This was belatedly recognized by the Obama administration itself. On the website announcing the passage of the "Every Student Succeeds Act," the Department of Education acknowledged that "over time, NCLB's prescriptive requirements became increasingly unworkable for schools and educators."[5] One White House press release decried the "one-size-fits-all mandates of the No Child Left Behind Act" and empowered "state and local decision-makers to develop their own strong systems for school improvement based upon evidence, rather than imposing cookie-cutter federal solutions like No Child Left Behind did."[6]

Quotations such as these from the very authorities that led the command and control strategies that it belatedly criticized indicate that the old *prescriptive imperative*, like the *ideological* and *imperial imperatives* before it, has exhausted itself. But exhaustion doesn't necessarily lead to change. It can just as likely lead to paralysis.

So a battle is underway now on a global scale for a new *professional imperative* that must be shaped by educators themselves. This has three components:

1 Educators must get smarter and better at the craft of teaching itself, both in their theoretical knowledge base and in practice.
2 Educators must develop their social capital through peer-learning networks that they themselves lead and control.
3 Educators must develop their autonomous judgment through constant inquiry, reflection, and improvement.

As stated in Chapter 1, this triple framing of the *professional imperative* augments the arguments for professional capital developed by Hargreaves and Fullan, along with the OECD's TALIS framework.[7] The two frameworks are depicted in Figure 4.1.

When brought together, these two frameworks provide powerful conceptual and evidence-based tools for improving teaching and learning.

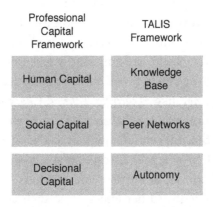

Figure 4.1 The Professional Capital and TALIS Frameworks Compared.

Deepening the Knowledge Base in Singapore

How should educators go about improving their knowledge base, or in the language of *Professional Capital*, their human capital? There is a wealth of research available now from world-renowned researchers and teachers. John Hattie's *Visible Learning*, to take one example, provides a panorama of over 800 meta-analyses drawn from over 50,000 studies on student achievement, with accompanying inferences for educators.[8] Doug Lemov's *Teaching Like a Champion* (2010) breaks teaching down into 49 practices that the author claims have lifted results.[9]

These are valuable contributions to the literature on teaching. Especially for beginning teachers, they contain a host of ideas on how to manage large and unruly classes of restless youngsters and how to get them focused on activities that will stretch their thinking far beyond memorization and recall. The videos that accompany *Teaching Like a Champion* online are full of practical advice on ways to introduce lessons, to pace them in a way that bring along struggling learners, and to evaluate students not only on state examinations but on a broader assortment of evaluations. This is done in a way that conveys an upbeat, can-do attitude that has contributed to their enormous popularity.

Lemov is weak on the empirical foundations of his strategies, beyond the success of the "Uncommon Schools" network in which he has been a leader. This could be questioned because the Uncommon Schools draw primarily on student results in high-achieving charter schools, and research continues to raise questions about how representative the students in such schools are.[10] Hattie's recommendations, on the other hand, are empirically grounded. What does he say about the best ways to improve teachers' knowledge base?

Invisible Learning, like *Teaching Like a Champion*, abounds in advice for classroom teachers. Educators are shown that some effect sizes measuring the impacts of different pedagogies are enormous. These are related to practices as diverse as classroom management styles, student feedback strategies, and teachers' clarity with their instructions to students. Other effect sizes, such as whole language, student control over learning, and out-of-school experiences such as field trips are minuscule. These effect sizes are listed in rank order online.[11] The implication appears to be clear: Teachers can maximize their students' learning by implementing practices with track records of success, as determined by effect sizes.

Or is it really so clear? Toward the end of *Invisible Learning*, Hattie cautions that "evidence based on effect sizes alone could lead to poor decisions" because every educational choice involves trade-offs, and some of the most important reforms related to teachers' professional development are expensive.[12] There is a belated recognition that it is necessary to balance different kinds of reforms with prosaic everyday realities related to school budgets, political pressures, and teachers' workplace cultures. Effect sizes, then, are advisory. They are not a dogma to be worshipped.

So books such as *Teaching Like a Champion* and *Invisible Learning* offer numerous strengths, but are necessarily incomplete. They focus so much on the intricacies of classroom teaching that they do not ask after aspects of teacher learning that could stretch across classrooms and schools. These are important because an excessively narrow definition of the profession has led teachers in many cases to define themselves as a "grade 4 teacher" or a "middle school math teacher," for example.

The best school system that socializes educators into a broad understanding of their profession is that of the small city-state of Singapore.[13] For some, it is absurd to imagine that a minuscule island at the tip of the Malay peninsula could have much to offer to larger systems. But skeptics need to be reminded that it was tiny Singapore that so impressed Chinese Premier Xiaopeng when he visited it in 1978 that he subsequently set about creating Special Economic Zones back home. These transformed the Peoples' Republic of China from an underdeveloped backwater to the world's largest economy in just 35 years.

Singapore's educational system has six strands that are especially striking in terms of their intense dedication to teaching and learning. First, Singaporean educators are guaranteed by their work contracts access to 100 hours of professional development each year. In no other system is there such a clear, explicit recognition that teaching is a complex profession and requires continual learning if it is to be honed to perfection. Policy makers in other jurisdictions need to be told, "Don't tell me about your values; just show me your budget allocations for your teachers' professional development."

Second, teachers in Singapore have the clearest professional development ladders of any system in the world. This is not based upon their students' test score results, but on a composite of indicators reflecting their strengths and the contributions that they can make to the school system. Early on, they are identified and recruited into career tracks that emphasize school leadership, teacher leadership, or curriculum development and support. This does not happen for one or two special teachers, but for all teachers. The system sends out the explicit message that continued professional learning and growth is not optional but obligatory.

Third, Singapore teachers use a term that I have never heard in the US. This is the term "seconded." In Singapore, this refers to when a teacher has been transferred for a few years to the National Institute of Education, where all teachers are prepared. The term "posted" is used when teachers are transferred to the Ministry of Education. Teachers are seconded and posted frequently because educators do not serve a particular subject, nor a particular school, but the profession. This requires that once they have accomplished a given level of practice they will move about in the system to circulate their knowledge and to learn from others. This is all done in a smoothly organized fashion that allows teachers to continue to progress in their career ladders. (This aspect of Singaporean professionalism is especially striking for me because I once had a large grant in the US in which I endeavored to work with colleagues to establish a similar level of professional fluidity among seven higher education institutions, 18 schools, and the Massachusetts Department of Elementary and Secondary Education. The bureaucratic barriers were too great. It didn't work.)

Fourth, the circulation of teachers is expedited by norms that communicate that every child truly matters for the future of Singapore and possesses strengths that cannot be wasted. Ironically, in ostensibly meritocratic Singapore, there is much more attentiveness to social justice in education than in many other allegedly democratic systems. It is common when visiting schools to meet educators who are working in the island's poorest communities who previously were posted in the most privileged schools. These educators consider it a badge of honor to be working in a community where their talents are most needed. For something similar to happen in a country like the US, it would need to be routine that educators from affluent suburban schools would be re-assigned to the inner city, and would be viewed by others as experts at the pinnacle of their powers.

Fifth, Singaporean educators have done a masterful job blending new technologies with the old. Ngee Ann Secondary School was developed by principal Adrian Lim into an award-winning technology school, but the first thing that I saw upon entering it several years ago wasn't a computer lab. Instead, I entered well-equipped art studios, in which students mastered calligraphy. Further on, I visited a design studio in which students created their own online art galleries and explored principles of robotics. Teachers encouraged students to use Twitter to post questions in real time on a screen at the front of the room, and they also used closed Facebook pages to post readings, track student discussions about course material, and to correct misconceptions.

When I asked Ngee Ann teachers how much they used new technologies in their instruction, they estimated between 20 and 30 percent. They were clear that they wanted their students to master a demanding academic curriculum, and that technology that distracted from that was forbidden. In the same school, Lim showed a powerful video clip as part of the school's professional development. It was entitled "Disconnect to Connect," and it urged viewers to put away their devices and to rediscover the importance of family and friends. This professional development asked educators to use technology intentionally and to put it away when it gets in the way of powerful experiences.

Sixth, Singaporean educators are intrigued but not blinded by test score results. This theme is vividly depicted in Pak Tee Ng's companion volume in this Routledge Leading Change Series entitled *Educational Change in Singapore: Drawing Strengths from Paradoxes*.[14] At a personal level, I've had the privilege of hosting delegations of Singaporean educators in the US, and have been impressed by the kinds of schools they want to visit. These include traditional inner-city public schools, Catholic suburban schools, and Waldorf schools. They don't make a beeline for charter schools. They know that there are many different kinds of schools available to learn from, and that doing so is part of their professional obligation for deepening their knowledge base.

No system is perfect, and Singaporean educators are resolutely modest about their schools. They are aware of the shortcoming caused by years of "kiasu," a local term referring to the fear of being left behind. This is a small country that was easily invaded and occupied by the Japanese during World War II. Even though the memories fade with every passing year, the anxiety persists.

To address the negative aspects of what is called "kiasuism," the Singaporean school system has been trying to open up more space for creativity through a policy of "Teach Less, Learn More." The professional knowledge that the TALIS framework calls for, and has been developed so well in the Singaporean system, thus will need to be understood in a flexible way. There is growing awareness that the knowledge base needs to expand beyond what is easily measured. As the system reinvents itself, so too should our ways of understanding its teachers' evolving professionalism.

Spreading Peer Learning Networks in Mexico

From its origin in medieval European universities to the present day, the concept of professionalism always has combined expert knowledge and public service. With the rise of modern government agencies, professionalism has become entangled with certification or accreditation of schools and universities. This can make the term "professional" sclerotic. When reduced to a series of atomized items on a checklist, the nobility of the enterprise is compromised. A calling that should inspire and transform, at least in part through the relationships between teachers and students, becomes all about compliance and consent.

A dynamic professionalism cannot give into these administrative tendencies, indispensable as they are. It must be recreated in new and unlikely settings with the original concepts of expertise and service recombined in new ways. To see how such a dynamic professionalism is taking shape, educators need to look beyond high-achieving jurisdictions in the affluent economies of the global North.

Latin America in particular is a region that today is a rich hybrid of indigenous cultures and European immigrants. Whatever influences are felt from outside, Latin America has preserved its own traditions. One of these is the idea of "de-schooling society."[15] This philosophy originated in the 1960s through intellectual exchanges at the Centro Intercultural de Documentación in Cuernavaca, Mexico. Gabriel Cámara, a young Mexican looking to develop his ideas, was one of those attracted to Cuernavaca at the time, where he was enthralled by a promising new vision of educational and societal change.

Like many reformers, Cámara's first realization of the many limitations of traditional schooling had come when he himself had been a student. He was having trouble with mathematics as a middle school pupil until a boy from his neighborhood offered to tutor him. With the little bit of extra assistance, Cámara came to excel in math: "I was surprised to learn that I was capable of learning and also of enjoying learning," he later wrote.[16]

Cámara never forgot this experience. Years later he and his colleagues created a network entitled the "Learning Community Project" (LCP). The LCP has spread a new model of tutorial relationships throughout schools. Participating schools improved results "at a similar or faster pace than schools not in the program" in Spanish and mathematics.[17] How has the LCP attained these results?

When I went to study the LCP in 2012, in one rural middle school students were seated across small tables from one another. One student was a tutor; another received tutoring. The selection of the tutor and the tutee was not ability-based in any traditional sense of the term but much more had to do with whether a given student had mastered enough of the curriculum to impart it to another. The curriculum was directly taken from the Ministry of Education in Mexico City. Tutors had learned to ask some kinds of questions related to a given curricular exercise but not others so that their knowledge could be developed logically from one step to the next. The learning atmosphere was intense but not stressed.

Tutors were not passive in this experience. They were charged with not just observing the students they were tutoring, but also with taking detailed notes on what they were observing about the learning process. They were taught by their teachers to practice mindful, critical engagement with the thinking of the student who is being tutored. Probing dialogue between tutor and tutee is encouraged, but the tutor must not give the tutee the answer to a question. The upshot is that while one student is learning the academic curriculum, the other student is studying learning—developing the skills of attentiveness to detail and the complex nature of problem solving that are required for mastering any discipline. All students, from the brightest to those who are most challenged, in this way are taught by their teachers how to learn and how to teach.

In too many schools, small group work is handled in a sloppy fashion. It's easy for students to distract one another and to get off task. One of the factors that makes tutorial relationships effective in Mexico concerns the ways in which new knowledge is shared with the whole school community. The conclusion of the tutoring is a public demonstration of content mastery. Students know that on occasion they will be called to stand before their peers or the faculty to show that they have mastered all of the steps in solving a problem.

When Cámara leads this process with students, teachers, and principals, it is fiercely rigorous. There is an intensity and focus to the questioning not seen in many presentations of student work. The presenter has to be prepared to defend the solution from multiple perspectives. Superficial knowledge of an answer is not enough. The tone is dialogical, but also critical, probing, and insistent. Question and answer fly back and forth in a way that is reminiscent of the intellectual training that Cámara himself internalized in his many years as a Jesuit priest.

Cámara and his colleagues discuss how important it is to master the subject matter so that learners are secure in their knowledge. The curriculum has to be struggled over and wrestled with before it can be internalized. This means that the learner has to be reconceptualized from being a passive recipient to an active inquirer. There are similarities here to Paolo Freire's "problem-posing" pedagogy, with the key difference that Freire focused exclusively on adult education in factories or fields.[18] Cámara has taken Freire's principles into schools. This is the opposite of de-schooling society. It is re-schooling it, with a different kind of professional logic at work.

With test scores rising in participating schools, state governments and the Ministry of Education in Mexico City provided funding to expand tutorial pedagogies to over 9,000 schools by 2012. Many of the newly participating schools were remote rural and severely under-funded middle schools with pedagogies that relied excessively on unimaginative frontal instruction on government-sponsored television programs for instruction. Tutorial relations in these schools transformed learning from passive listening to active engagement. Students and teachers responded with enthusiasm. Over 43 regional exchanges occurred across schools to spread the pedagogy, along with two national "Learning Fairs" in Mexico City and Querétaro.

During a visit to an urban secondary school in 2012, I found over one hundred teachers working in tutorial pairs on mathematics cur-riculum to fortify their understanding. I circulated freely throughout the transformed school gymnasium, approaching learners in disparate corners of the room to get a sense of just how genuine the tutorial process was. Discussions with the teachers revealed a calm and focused engagement with learning. Those who had struggled with concepts they were required to teach were especially grateful for the tutorial experience. Experienced teachers know that there is nothing more frustrating than feeling insecure in one's own academic content knowledge. Tutorial relations gave teachers a humanistic foundation for consolidating their knowledge from a sympathetic and supportive colleague. Tutorial relations are transforming professional develop-ment in Mexico, with implications for educators everywhere.

As tutorial relations spread through Mexico, its practices became powerful because of their popularity. In this way tutorial relations became a social movement with a strong foundation, especially in rural schools. The LCP's egalitarian message challenged the tradi-tional culture of schools with their clear definitions of control and hierarchy. Power in Spanish is *poder*, which means "to be able to" in the sense of capacity. "The important point was not only taking power, but also changing its logic," Rincón-Gallardo has written.[19] Power in tutorial relations is a precondition for improved learning.

At times, government authorities in Mexico have become con-cerned that they had empowered schools working with the LCP beyond what originally had been intended. Funding lines were then cut as authorities sought to re-establish traditional definitions of schooling. When the Ministry of Education cut funding, educators responded with initiatives at the state level. When funding has been reduced in some states, tutorial network leaders have relocated to others.

Although poverty is more pervasive in Mexico than in most of North America and Europe, tutorial educators have had some advantages over educators in other jurisdictions. State examinations have been suspended since 2013, which has enabled educators to preserve the key principle of enabling students to learn at their own pace rather than in highly pressurized environments. Even when government endeavors to be prescriptive, it lacks the resources for surveillance, so educators have the freedom to experiment. The states of Guanajuato, Veracruz, Durango, and Chiapas continue to support regional exchanges of schools participating in tutorial relationships.

The model developed by Cámara and his colleagues of tutorial relationships in Mexico has been spread across the country and recently has been taken up by 60 schools in Chile. It demonstrates the power of peer learning networks to transform the teaching and learning that is at the heart of education. This is a new form of professionalism. It is not based upon teachers' power over their students. It is based on a common pursuit of understanding.

Enhancing Mindful Teaching in Arizona

Today some of the most inspiring work I know of regarding teacher learning is occurring in a US state with one of the lowest per-pupil expenditures: Arizona. This southwestern state has never been generous with its students or its teachers. Professional associations are weak. It is easy to circumvent the regulatory safeguards in place by many states if anyone, with just the minimum of professional training, wants to open up a charter school or home school children. Arizona receives a grade of D+ on the Quality Counts Report of the Education Week Research Center, which ranks the Grand Canyon state 47th out of all 50 on its overall state grade.[20]

Educators have endeavored to improve schools in Arizona, in part by creating innovative curricula to engage the many immigrant and

Latino students with studies of their own culture. These, however, provoked a backlash by politicians concerned that they were sponsoring ethnic separatism. Arizona in 2010 banned a popular Mexican-American studies course from the curricular offerings in Tucson. A state audit later indicated that there was no evidence supporting the contention of ethnic chauvinism. A careful empirical study showed that students who took the course had higher grade point averages and a higher graduation rate than a control group.[21]

In Arizona the supports provided by the state and school districts are weak for professionals. The politics of education are adversarial and project a divided public. What of promise could be going on in regard to teachers' learning in Arizona?

The Arizona K12 Center provides a resource that shows how creative and persistent leadership can uplift the teaching profession even in contested circumstances. For 15 years the state's teachers have organized their work collectively under the auspices of the Center. Unlike many non-profit organizations that are beholden to the shifting winds of funders and policy makers, the Center has served as the conscience of the profession in challenging times.

When teacher leader Daniela Robles organized staff at her school to undertake school-wide licensure by the National Board for Professional Teaching Standards (NBPTS), she was prepared for hard work. She was not prepared for her district to re-assign her to another school as a consequence. Thanks to the Center, Robles' experiences, as well as those of her colleagues, were captured in a film, "The Mitchell 20," that documents the roadblocks facing teachers who want to get better at their craft.[22]

The Arizona K12 Center defines a core part of its mandate as developing teacher leaders while providing the supports they need to keep them in the classroom. It has done this by developing a "Teacher Solutions Team" that is available to mentor other teachers and that actively posts on a blog entitled "Stories from School AZ."[23] The blog provides a space for teachers to ask one another critical questions about what is happening with their profession. Postings reveal educators at their best: As witty provocateurs of student learning who are willing to exhaust every strategy and more to help reluctant and oppositional students to achieve.

Among the questions posed by educators on "Stories from School" are the following:

- Why have policies at the state and federal level required students to take ten hours of standardized tests in ten days, instead of trusting teachers to keep track of their students' learning?
- Why do journalists who never taught high school and don't appreciate the stability it can provide for those from turbulent home environments get so much attention by calling for its abolition?
- Why have experienced teachers with so much to offer had to go to the same mind-numbing presentations about how to close out the academic calendar year after year?
- Why are students recruited to sell overpriced frozen meats as fund-raisers for their schools, and then, when they don't bring in expected revenues, this task is passed on to teachers?

You'd have to have a heart of stone not to be moved by these teachers' motivation to get past the mountains of distractions that stand in their pathways in order to do the best they can for their students. You'd have to be deaf to teachers' voices not to heed their call for a recalibration of how we organize our schools and how we should relate to our students. There is little in the "Stories from School" about benefits to education from policies that teachers received from on high. Instead, there are accounts of struggling students and steadfast educators working hand in hand in a joint effort to attain achievement with integrity.

The Arizona K12 Center, like the LCP, gives educators the space they crave for learning how to make the best possible judgments for their students. This is described as "decisional capital" in the professional capital framework and "autonomy" in the TALIS framework. The Arizona teachers use the term "mindful teaching" to capture the reflective and intellectual components of their craft. They have compiled a report, "Mindful Teacher Leadership in Arizona Schools and Communities," that describes this work.[24] Drawing upon my research with Boston Public Schools teacher leader Elizabeth MacDonald, the report provides anchoring illustrations of how teachers' professional judgment is exercised on behalf of their students.[25] These include the following:

- Deborah Kohls advocated for a struggling student with behavioral problems for years after he had left her elementary school classroom, including at his middle school, because she knew that without her support, he would be lost without an ally in the larger school.
- Treva Jenkins battled to retain a popular curriculum resource when district funding for the materials was cut because she saw how it benefited her students.
- Melanie Volz and her colleagues at Playa del Rey Elementary School in Gilbert Public Schools determined that they have the talent and resources to develop a teacher-led school that will focus on students' learning when making all decisions in their building.

In the above cases and those of the other anchoring illustrations, Arizona's educators prove that one should never wait to exercise what is called either decisional capital or autonomy. With the support of colleagues at the Arizona K12 Center, mindful teacher leadership is exhibited when educators step forward to advocate on behalf of their students, to choose the very best curricula, and to redesign school leadership in ways that focus more on learning and less on management. They are new manifestations of professionalism for educators. They do not circumvent the profession from without. They build it up from within.

Conclusion

New repertoires for deepening teachers' knowledge base in Singapore, spreading peer learning networks in Mexico, and cultivating mindful teacher leadership in Arizona reveal facets of a new professionalism for teachers. This is activist and innovative rather than data-driven or compliance-oriented. It is bold and specific. It is reflective rather than reactive. Such emerging models of change reflect an explosion of innovation in the education sector. There are sites where achievement with integrity is enacted in an exemplary fashion.

In the TALIS 2013 study, the authors note that "in many countries, external accountability for professionalism has created a 'prescribed' professionalism dictated by national policies and standards, which differs from the 'enacted' professionalism that exists in teachers' practices."[26] They are emphatic that prescribed professionalism is a dead end. Nations that are serious about long-term, sustainable change give their teachers an excellent knowledge base, strong peer networks, and the autonomy to make good decisions.

The TALIS study represents the work of the OECD at its very best. The findings are crystal clear. An older *prescriptive imperative* would have educators complying with government policies even when everyday observations of student learning indicate that there are better ways to teach. This is the cul-de-sac of alienated teaching. Its resolution is a new *professional imperative*:

1   Teachers must get smarter and better at the core tasks of teaching and learning, as is done on a system-wide level in Singapore.
2   Teachers must participate in peer networks that circulate knowledge around about uplifting pedagogies, as is done with the LCP in Mexico.
3   Teachers must recover professional judgment in ways that promote student learning and restore dignity and wonder to the heart of the enterprise, as is done by the teachers in Arizona.

These triple components provide openings for a newly revitalized professionalism. But they are incomplete insofar as each remains bounded within national constraints. In a world of instantaneous communication across countries educators can't be limited by national policies. They need a broader vision of cosmopolitan humanism that encompasses and advocates for all of the world's children and youth. How we do this in a way that uplifts our students and their learning is the subject of the next chapter.

Notes

1   OECD (2014) *TALIS 2013 results: An international perspective on teaching and learning.* Paris: OECD.
2   Shirley, D., & MacDonald, E. (2016) *The mindful teacher.* New York: Teachers College Press.
3   Shirley & MacDonald, *The mindful teacher*, p. 3.
4   Stone-Johnson, C. (2016) Intensification and isolation: Alienated teaching and collaborative professional relationships in the accountability context. *Journal of Educational Change* 17(1), 29–50.

5 Retrieved from www.ed.gov/essa?src=rn.
6 Retrieved from www.whitehouse.gov/the-press-office/2015/12/03/fact-sheet-congress-acts-fix-no-child-left-behind.
7 Hargreaves, A., & Fullan, M. (2012) *Professional capital: Transforming teaching in every school*. New York: Teachers College Press. Schleicher, A. (2016) *Teaching excellence through professional learning and policy reform: Lessons from around the world*. Paris: OECD.
8 Hattie, J. (2009) *Visible learning: A synthesis of 800 meta-analyses relating to achievement*. New York: Routledge.
9 Lemov, D. (2010) *Teach like a champion: 49 techniques that put students on the path to college (K-12)*. San Francisco: Jossey-Bass.
10 Heilig, J.V., Williams, A., McNeil, L.M., & Lee, C. (2011) Is choice a panacea? An analysis of black secondary student attrition from KIPP, other private charters, and urban districts. *Berkeley Review of Education* 2(2), 153–178.
11 Go to visible-learning.org.
12 Hattie, *Visible learning*, p. 255.
13 This discussion builds on research Andy Hargreaves and I published in 2012 in *The global fourth way: The quest for educational excellence*. Thousand Oaks, CA: Corwin. See also my C.J. Koh lecture entitled *Achieving with integrity: Towards mindful educational change* (2014) Singapore: National Institute of Education, Singapore. Retrieved from www.nie.edu.sg/research/publication/cj-koh-professional-lecture.
14 Ng, P.T. (2016) *Educational change in Singapore: Drawing strength from paradoxes*. New York: Routledge.
15 Illich, I. (1970) *Deschooling society*. New York: Harper & Row.
16 Cámara, G. (2008) *Otra educación básica es posible* [A different basic education is possible]. Mexico City: Siglo XXI.
17 Rincón-Gallardo, S. (forthcoming, 2016) Large-scale pedagogical transformation as widespread cultural change in Mexican public schools. *Journal of Educational Change*.
18 Freire, P. (2000) *Pedagogy of the oppressed*. New York: Continuum.
19 Rincón-Gallardo, S. (2015) Bringing a counter-hegemonic pedagogy to scale in Mexican public schools. *Multidisciplinary Journal of Educational Research* 5(1), 38–54, quote from p. 48.
20 *Education Week* (2016, January 26) Quality counts 2016: State report cards map. *Education Week*. Retrieved from www.edweek.org/ew/qc/2016/2016-state-report-cards-map.html.
21 Cabrera, N.L., Milem, J.F., Jaquette, O., & Marx, R.W. (2014) Missing the (student achievement) forest for all the (political trees): Empiricism and the Mexican American studies controversy in Tucson. *American Educational Research Journal* 51(4), 1084–1118.
22 Retrieved from www.mitchell20.com/.
23 Retrieved from www.storiesfromschoolaz.org.
24 Arizona K12 Center (2015) *Mindful teacher leadership in Arizona schools and communities*. Phoenix: Arizona K12 Center. Retrieved from http://azk12.org/sites/default/files/attachments/AZK1508_MindfulTeacherLeadershipReport_v8_060115_web_0.pdf.
25 Shirley and MacDonald, *The mindful teacher*.
26 OECD (2016) *Supporting teacher professionalism: Insights from TALIS 2013*. Paris: OECD, p. 27. The distinction made between "prescribed" and "enacted" professionalism is drawn from Evans, L. (2008) Professionalism, professionality and the development of education professionals. *British Journal of Educational Studies* 56(1), 20–38.

References

Arizona K12 Center (2015) *Mindful teacher leadership in Arizona schools and communities*. Phoenix: Arizona K12 Center. Retrieved from http://azk12.org/sites/default/files/attachments/AZK1508_MindfulTeacherLeadershipReport_v8_060115_web_0.pdf.

Cabrera, N.L., Milem, J.F., Jaquette, O., & Marx, R.W. (2014) Missing the (student achievement) forest for all the (political) trees: Empiricism and the Mexican American studies controversy in Tucson. *American Educational Research Journal* 51(4), 1084–1118.

Cámara, G. (2008) *Otra educación básica es posible* [A different basic education is possible]. Mexico City: Siglo XXI.

Education Week (2016, January 26) Quality counts 2016: State report cards map. *Education Week*. Retrieved from www.edweek.org/ew/qc/2016/2016-state-report-cards-map.html.

Evans, L. (2008) Professionalism, professionality and the development of education professionals. *British Journal of Educational Studies* 56(1), 20–38.

Freire, P. (2000) *Pedagogy of the oppressed*. New York: Continuum.

Hargreaves, A., & Fullan, M. (2012) *Professional capital: Transforming teaching in every school*. New York: Teachers College Press.

Hargreaves, A., & Shirley, D. (2012) *The global fourth way: The quest for educational excellence*. Thousand Oaks, CA: Corwin.

Hattie, J. (2009) *Visible learning: A synthesis of 800 meta-analyses relating to achievement*. New York: Routledge.

Heilig, J.V., Williams, A., McNeil, L.M., & Lee, C. (2011) Is choice a panacea? An analysis of black secondary student attrition from KIPP, other private charters, and urban districts. *Berkeley Review of Education* 2(2), 153–178.

Illich, I. (1970) *Deschooling society*. New York: Harper & Row.

Lemov, D. (2010) *Teach like a champion: 49 techniques that put students on the path to college (K–12)*. San Francisco: Jossey-Bass.

Ng, P.T. (2016) *Educational change in Singapore: Drawing strength from paradoxes*. New York: Routledge.

OECD (2014) *TALIS 2013 results: An international perspective on teaching and learning*. Paris: OECD.

OECD (2016) *Supporting teacher professionalism: Insights from TALIS 2013*. Paris: OECD.

Rincón-Gallardo, S. (2015) Bringing a counter-hegemonic pedagogy to scale in Mexican public schools. *Multidisciplinary Journal of Educational Research* 5(1), 38–54, quote from p. 48.

Rincón-Gallardo, S. (forthcoming, 2016) Large-scale pedagogical transformation as widespread cultural change in Mexican public schools. *Journal of Educational Change*.

Schleicher, A. (2016) *Teaching excellence through professional learning and policy reform: Lessons from around the world*. Paris: OECD.

Shirley, D. (2014) *Achieving with integrity: Towards mindful educational change.* Singapore: National Institute of Education, Singapore. Retrieved from www.nie.edu.sg/research/publication/cj-koh-professional-lecture.

Shirley, D., & MacDonald, E. (2016) *The mindful teacher.* New York: Teachers College Press.

Stone-Johnson, C. (2016) Intensification and isolation: Alienated teaching and collaborative professional relationships in the accountability context. *Journal of Educational Change* 17(1), 29–50.

5

THE GLOBAL IMPERATIVE

OPTIMIZING CONVERGENCE

Scotland rests on the northern border with England. While it shares any number of similar policies with England as part of the United Kingdom, in education Scotland has endeavored to pursue different policies. As an aggregate, these have led to higher results on PISA. It would seem obvious that the English would be curious about what is going on with their northern neighbors, and would send delegations up to adapt elements from Scotland for their own schools. What independent Scottish educational policies have the English tried out? None.

Sweden shares a common border with Finland, also a high achiever on PISA. Finland's school policies have been the polar opposite of the market-based strategies pursued by Sweden, and has become a must-see travel destination for school reformers the world over. What Finnish policies have the Swedes taken over? None.

Extending 5,525 miles, the US has the world's longest border with Canada, another country that has done well on PISA. Over 90 percent of Canadians live within 100 miles of the US, making the overwhelming majority of their schools easily accessible for visitors from south of the border. What Canadian policies have been transferred into the US? None.

For all of the chatter about data-driven decision-making that has gone on for years now, an *insular imperative* has characterized many nations. Their policy makers have been tone deaf. They have persisted with strategies that have not lifted student achievement. Such policy makers have failed to learn from nations that have performed better, even when they share geographical proximity, a common language, and cultural similarities.

Why is this? It's hard not to think that long-standing and deeply ingrained attitudes of one country toward another play a role. The English economy is larger than the Scottish one. The same can be said about the Swedes in relation to the Finns or the US in relation to Canada. Countries that lead in economic clout appear to have a hard time admitting that they might learn from others who do better in education. It's easier to be insular.

The old *insular imperative* is related to the *imperious imperative* in paradoxical ways. How can an imperious stance be connected with insularity at one and the same time? This is possible if a nation projects its own policies and practices abroad for others to learn from while failing to model the position of a curious and open-minded learner in its own conduct. It is possible if a nation assumes that the answers to change all lie on one side, and that others, perhaps smaller and less powerful, have little to impart. It's hard not to connect a certain arrogance to the ways that the imperious and insular imperatives have interacted over the years. This would not matter so much at a purely political level, if students were not the ones who pay the price in terms of lost learning opportunities. It would not matter on the level of theory if teachers did not suffer from a sense of diminished professionalism in practice.

While educational policy makers in some nations have been strangely cut off from learning and trying out new strategies that they've acquired from across borders, what has been happening in other sectors?

AnnaLee Saxenian's study of digital entrepreneurs in *The New Argonauts: Regional Advantage in a Global Economy* provides one example.[1] In recent years computer engineers from India, Israel, and Taiwan have developed thousands of thriving new businesses as they connect labor demand in their home countries with technical expertise in Silicon Valley. "Brain drain" is out. "Brain gain" is in, with everyone benefiting through new jobs and greater prosperity.

Silicon Valley in California is the hub of this burgeoning new industry that is transforming everything from how we communicate to how we shop. If you're a technology entrepreneur in New Delhi or

Tel Aviv, you book a flight to San Francisco for meetings a few times a year to be sure, but you don't have to live there. You go to the Bay area to get new information to take back, circulate, and capitalize upon on your home turf. It's all about gaining new knowledge, moving it around with colleagues, and then making the most of it collectively—just as it should be for the professionals in our schools today.

With all of this dynamism, to seek to contain education within standardized boundaries in a constricted curriculum with principals who are nailed down doing endless paperwork is to give in to an outdated *insular imperative*. Fortunately, educators don't have to start from scratch. In the remainder of this chapter I first will describe a vision for global education that has been produced by the United Nations Educational, Scientific and Cultural Organization (UNESCO) in three reports over many years that provides a humanistic understanding of the profession and its impact. Second, I will present a rights-based approach that is being used by transnational organizations as a moral anchor and political strategy to contain the worst aspects of globalization while making the most of its potential. Third, I will delineate strategies being pursued by Education International, the largest professional organization in the world with over 32 million educators, to advance a new change agenda. This encompasses the needs of students and teachers in both economically developed and developing nations.

Learning: The Treasure Within

In 1972 UNESCO released a report by an international team convened by lead author Edgar Faure, entitled *Learning to Be: The World of Education Today and Tomorrow.*[2] The Faure Report focused on the skills, aptitudes, and dispositions that young people would need to master the challenges of the late twentieth century. At no point in *Learning to Be* did the authors propose that educators should prioritize the creation of market systems that would rank students, schools, or countries against another.

Instead, *Learning to Be* called for an education that would promote "the fundamental solidarity of governments and peoples, despite transitory differences and conflicts."[3] This kind of education would advocate "belief in democracy" with education as its "keystone."[4] The Faure Report urged educators to promote the solidarity of peoples across cultures. It encouraged everyone to educate toward "the complete fulfillment" of each person "as individual, member of a family and of a community, citizen and producer, inventor of techniques, and creative dreamer."[5] Ultimately, the report affirmed, "We should no longer assiduously acquire knowledge once and for all, but learn how to build up a continually evolving body of knowledge all through life—'learn to be.'"[6]

In 1996 UNESCO issued a second report that was written by representatives of 15 nations. Its lead author was Jacque Delors, a former president of the European Commission. The "Delors Commission Report," as it came to be known, argued for four pillars for twenty-first-century education. Unlike today's prevalent approach to twenty-first-century skills, the report didn't begin with the state of the market and the required labor force for global economies. Instead, it argued that

> The far-reaching changes in the traditional patterns of life require of us a better understanding of other people and the world at large; they demand mutual understanding, peaceful interchange and indeed, harmony—the very things that are most lacking in our world today.[7]

This is a very different message from ones that argue for human capital development or for entrepreneurship. Alarmed by international conflicts, the authors emphasized the importance of *"learning to live together."* This would be pursued by

> creating a new spirit which, guided by recognition of our growing interdependence and a common analysis of the risks and challenges of the future, would induce people to implement common projects or to manage the inevitable conflicts in an intelligent and peaceful way.[8]

Educators were called upon to cultivate a new cosmopolitan solidarity within and across cultures.

The first pillar of international solidarity was to be supplemented by "three other pillars of education that provide, as it were, the bases for learning to live together."[9] These were:

- *learning to know*, which corresponds to the academic purposes of schools;
- *learning to do*, to make a practical contribution to society; and
- *learning to be* in a world in which "everyone will need to exercise greater independence and judgment combined with a stronger sense of personal responsibility for the attainment of common goals."[10] Finally, the report stressed that "none of the talents which are hidden like buried treasure in every person must be left untapped."[11]

The Delors Commission Report was entitled *Learning: The Treasure Within*. It has been published in more than 30 languages.[12] Here was international consensus among representatives of the world's people. Its message was clear: In a new millennium it isn't going to be enough to know how to memorize facts nor will it be enough to be able to make new products. Rather, we also need to ask: How should we be together? How should we show not only compassion, but also real solidarity with one another? How should we demonstrate an ethic of care in all that we do, while supporting the rights of others to lead their lives with autonomy and dignity? Finally, the Commission asked, how should we *be* as individuals? How can we assure that the lives of our young people have depth, avoiding what the report called "a society of the ephemeral and the immediate"?[13]

The Delors Commission Report reminded us that education is "primordial" in its moral content.[14] One cannot evade this moral content without mutilating the human spirit and our aspirations to live in peace with one another. Years in the making, the report demonstrated that representatives of diverse nations in an international body such as UNESCO could find common language and develop shared aspirations. *Learning: The Treasure Within* expanded the horizons of education beyond *knowing* and *doing* toward *being* and *being with others*. Its language encouraged educators and citizens the world over to re-imagine our prospects for a shared humanism in a new millennium.

In 2015, a third UNESCO report was published, entitled *Rethinking Education: Towards a Global Common Good?* It acknowledged and asserted that "The Delors Report was aligned closely with the moral principles that underpin UNESCO, and therefore its analysis and recommendations were more humanistic and less instrumental and market-driven than other education and reform studies of the time."[15] Repudiating the equation of education with human capital, *Rethinking Education* reaffirmed the "humanistic and holistic approach to education" advanced in the earlier reports and asked that educators create a "new development model" in which "economic growth must be guided by environmental stewardship and by concern for peace, inclusion, and social justice."[16]

The report celebrated areas of human progress in recent decades, observing that "Global rates of poverty declined by half between 1990 and 2010," largely because of the growth of emerging economies.[17] With over 90 percent of young people between the ages of 18 and 24 on some form of social media, the report said that new technologies have created "the most informed, active, connected, and mobile generation the world has ever seen."[18] Furthermore, it noted, mobility has reached unprecedented rates, with roughly one of every seven people—approximating one billion altogether—in one form or another "on the move."

What does this mean for educators? We are in situations of greater complexity than ever before, because "although economic activity is increasingly globalized, political decision-making and action remain essentially at the national level."[19] Educators struggle to socialize students into national identities but students' subjective life experiences increasingly are transnational, with their family members and friends drawn from many countries.[20] If we are skillful, our students can help us to optimize the convergence of cultures. If we fail to address the new *global imperative*, the young will find their educators unaware of the great transformations of our time.

The three UNESCO reports provide a powerful and intellectually rigorous response to the old imperatives of educational change that have become so influential in the past decades. Unlike the OECD, UNESCO represents not just affluent countries, but all nations. For many of these nations, the identification of children solely as carriers of human capital is not only culturally alien but also unethical.

The Rights of the Child

On their own, however, reports are toothless. They can exhort but they cannot compel. They are not legally binding. It is necessary to ensure that children have rights backed up by action. The idea of children's rights is not new. The first Declaration of the Rights of the Child was endorsed by the League of Nations in Geneva in 1924 in the wake of the horrors of World War I. This was refined and adopted by the United Nations General Assembly in New York in 1959 in the aftermath of World War II. On the thirtieth anniversary of the UN Declaration, it was expanded into an International Convention of the Rights of the Child.

Only one country, the United States, has not ratified the International Convention, of all member nations of the United Nations. Article 37 of the Convention forbids sentencing youth under 18 years old to life imprisonment without parole or the death penalty, which would put some US states out of compliance. That the world's only superpower has withheld its assent is a failure of leadership.

Overwhelming international consensus exists on the rights of the child. No other human rights document has been ratified by so many nations so quickly. The rights specified by the Convention include the "inherent right to life," "the right of the child to education," and the "right of the child to rest and leisure, to engage in play and recreational activities appropriate to the age of the child and to participate freely in cultural life and the arts."[21] In addition, children shall "be provided the opportunity to be heard" and they "shall have the right to freedom of expression" along with the right to "freedom of association and peaceful assembly."[22]

In practice, almost every nation falls short of the Convention's goals. Signatories to the Convention submit periodic reports to a UN Committee on the Rights of the Child, but governments can misrepresent the nature of children's rights by focusing on promulgations of policy rather than real evidence of societal progress. Over 59 million children of primary school age are out of school, in blatant violation of the Convention.[23] More than 168 million children of school age are engaged in child labor, which also is forbidden by the Convention.[24] In dozens of dictatorships adults, let alone children, are routinely arrested for such simple acts as reading benign but none-theless censored texts or holding minority religious beliefs.

Human rights activists, however, do not give up. In 2011 an Optional Protocol to the Convention was adopted by the General Assembly of the UN to empower children and their advocates to bring cases to the UN Committee on the Rights of the Child when they have been unable to secure redress for their grievances from their governments.[25] A global citizen campaign is underway to accelerate the Sustainable Development Goals of the UN for 2030, including the right to a quality education.[26] International organizations like Action Aid use a human rights based approach to their campaigns that assists local and indigenous peoples in their advocacy.[27] New technologies are bringing coherence and direction to the attainment of the goals.[28] By blending together greater efficacy for the UN and other transnational organizations along with the power of social movements and new technologies, the goal of a quality education for every child could be achieved early, laying the foundation for a more prosperous and equitable future for all.

Is there a role that educators can play in creating a global human rights movement for children? If so, can it be something more than that taken on by individuals acting solely out of their own good will?

Creating an International Educational Profession

To seek to be a professional without a professional association to represent you is to fail to understand collective action. It is to ask others to take on the role of representing you. Educators have a role to play in advancing the values established by the UNESCO reports and the Convention of the Rights of the Child.

Educators, like professionals around the world, are experiencing a massive restructuring of the economy that makes for an increasingly precarious future. Traditional understandings of job security and safeguards such as tenure that protected educators from capricious attacks are being eroded. They are being replaced with what *Rethinking Education* describes as "the casualization of teachers" through short-term contracts with low wages.[29] This "vulnerable employment" is not restricted to the education sector alone. It currently accounts for close to half of the total employment for workers globally.[30]

This is where the umbrella agency of professional associations from around the world—Education International—plays a significant role. Based in Brussels, Belgium, Education International represents 32.5 million educators from 393 member organizations in 196 countries.[31] Professional associations such as the American Federation of Teachers, the Australian Education Union, the Canadian Education Association, and the Union of Educators Norway are all affiliated with Education International.

These professional associations are engaged in an uphill battle to strengthen public education as a fundamental human right around the globe. They focus on their home countries but their ambit is much larger. Among other goals, they seek to bring the principles of the UNESCO reports to life.

About one-third of Education International's member organizations come from dues-paying nations in the developed world. Some of these nations have well-developed school systems, functioning ministries of education, and their own research infrastructures. Even if they are suffering from the long-term consequences of the recent economic recession, their citizens have the rights of freedom of speech and assembly, with the rule of law and due process. Many of these countries are democratic, and while they are flawed and with ample room for improvement, they nonetheless have vibrant social movements in place to strengthen human rights. They provide the lion's share of Education International's funding. This is essential not only for their own members, who often have to wrestle with the old imperatives in their systems, but also to support participation from poorer countries.

We know less about how well students in poorer nations are learning on international comparisons. Only 65 jurisdictions took the OECD's PISA test in 2012, although there are 197 nations. Only South Africa has participated in PISA of all of the sub-Saharan nations. Most of India and China, the world's two most populous countries, have not participated at all outside of a scattering of cities or states. Given this variation, PISA cannot provide a truly global ranking of education systems.

In many countries teachers' professional associations have a precarious existence. Their leaders face imprisonment if they speak out for educators' rights. Because a large proportion of the education sector in the developing world is often reliant on external funding, these nations are susceptible to imported models of marketplace competition and technology-driven change from organizations like the World Bank.

It is the historical responsibility of Education International to develop strategies to advance the teaching profession along three lines. First, Education International strives to defend public educational systems in the developed world. Without such a defense it cannot maintain its revenues or grow its membership. Second, it conducts advocacy and provides support for children without schooling in the developing world. It has done this by ensuring that education is prominent in the Sustainable Development Goals of the United Nations. Third, it creates advocacy networks within and across nations to improve the quality of schooling. These have become increasingly important as governments may endorse the International Convention of the Rights of the Child in theory, but fail to maintain its principles in practice.

Fred van Leeuwen, General Secretary of Education International, has long promoted international solidarity among educators and especially promoted the social values of democracy, inclusion, and equity in schools. National professional associations have augmented this awareness and advocacy. Randi Weingarten, President of the American Federation of Teachers (AFT), has spoken out on behalf of educators in Argentina, Brazil, and the Ukraine in recent visits.[32] Likewise, the National Education Association (NEA) in the US for many years has supported the rights of educators and students around the world, from advocating for the founding of UNESCO in 1945 to a call for global competencies as a twenty-first-century imperative. President Lily Eskelsen-García of the NEA has been following international studies closely and has skillfully described what is accurate and what could be misread from such research.[33] The Canadian Teachers' Federation has long supported international educational exchanges and work abroad to support the profession in emerging economies.[34] Angelo

Gavrielatos, former President of the Australian Education Union, currently is Project Director of an Educational International group organizing a global professional response to the commercialization of education.[35] These kinds of activities help educators everywhere to develop into global citizens.

When we ask what it would take for our students to be successful, we need to take a long-term and also humanistic perspective as well as an economic one. The Human Development Report of 2010 that is written by the UN Development Program revealed phenomenal progress in levels of education in almost every country since 1970. The exceptions were in war-torn regions. If a country avoids military conflict, it is virtually certain that educational gains ensue.[36]

We should draw hope from the evidence that the world has been making progress. The percentage of the world's population that lives on less than $1.25 per day declined from 40 percent in 1981 to 14 percent in 2010. The first Millennium Development Goal—to halve the world's population living in extreme poverty by 2015—was met five years early.[37]

How can we further advance the improvement of the human condition through education? Since October 2013 Education International has been working with UNESCO and UNICEF to promote the "Quality for Education" campaign for excellent teachers, materials, and settings for the world's children.[38] Education International has launched an initiative entitled "The World's Largest Lesson" in partnership with UNICEF to develop a curriculum promoting leadership for the Sustainable Development Goals.[39] It is because of Education International's advocacy that "quality education" is ranked as the fourth of the 17 goals.[40] These are major international initiatives everyone should support.

In a world of increasing economic interdependence and cross-cultural exchange educators no longer can be satisfied with the constraints of an older and long outmoded *insular imperative*. The *global imperative* requires that educators avail themselves of opportunities to create a united profession wherever their schools are located. If academic achievement can be raised in the right ways, students will not only learn to know, as the Delors Commission Report espoused, or how to do things that contribute to a better world. They will also learn how to be together by serving on diverse teams that straddle the world's cultures.

Still, one important goal of the Delors Commission Report has not been addressed. What role should educators and schools play in learning to be? This is the subject of the fifth, *existential imperative* of educational change.

Notes

1 Saxenian, A. (2006) *The new argonauts: Regional advantage in a global economy.* Cambridge, MA: Harvard University Press.
2 Faure, E., Herrera, F., Kaddoura, A., Lopes, H., Petrovsky, A., Rahnema, M., & Ward, F.C. (1972) *Learning to be: The world of education today and tomorrow.* Paris: UNESCO.
3 Faure et al., *Learning to be*, p. vi.
4 Faure et al., *Learning to be*, p. vi.
5 Faure et al., *Learning to be*, p. vi.
6 Faure et al., *Learning to be*, p. vi.
7 Delors, J., et al. (1996) *Learning: The treasure within.* Paris: UNESCO, p. 22.
8 Delors et al., *Learning*, p. 22.
9 Delors et al., *Learning*, p. 23.
10 Delors et al., *Learning*, p. 23.
11 Delors et al., *Learning*, p. 23.
12 Draxler, A. (2010) The Delors commission and report. Geneva: Graduate Institute of International and Development Studies. Retrieved from www.norrag.org/es/publications/boletin-norrag/online-version/a-world-of-reports-a-critical-review-of-global-development-reports-with-an-angle-on-education-and-training/detail/the-delors-commission-and-report.html.
13 Delors et al., *Learning*, p. 66.
14 Delors et al., *Learning*, p. 188.
15 UNESCO (2015) *Rethinking education: Towards a global common good?* Paris: UNESCO, p. 15.
16 UNESCO, *Rethinking education*, p. 10.
17 UNESCO, *Rethinking education*, p. 22.
18 UNESCO, *Rethinking education*, p. 28.
19 UNESCO, *Rethinking education*, p. 58.
20 Skerrett, A. (2015) *Teaching transnational youth: Literacy and education in a changing world.* New York: Teachers College Press.
21 United Nations General Assembly (1990) Convention on the rights of the child. Part 1, Article 31. Retrieved from www.ohchr.org/en/professionalinterest/pages/crc.aspx.
22 United Nations General Assembly, Convention on the rights of the child. Part 1, Articles 12 and 13.
23 UNESCO Institute for Statistics (2015) *A growing number of children and adolescents are out of school as aid fails to meet the mark.* Policy Paper 22/Fact Sheet 31, p. 1. Retrieved from http://unesdoc.unesco.org/images/0023/002336/233610e.pdf.
24 International Labor Office (2015) *Making progress against child labor: Global estimates and trends, 2000–2012.* Geneva: International Labor Office, p. 9.
25 UNICEF (2014, May 14) *Convention on the rights of the child: Advancing the CRC.* Retrieved from www.unicef.org/crc/index_protocols.html.

26 Go to globalcitizen.org.
27 Go to www.actionaid.org.
28 Go to www.connecttheworld.org.
29 UNESCO, *Rethinking education*, p. 54.
30 International Labor Office (2014) *Global employment trends 2014*. Geneva: International Labor Office.
31 Retrieved from www.ei-ie.org/en/.
32 Pechthalt, J. (2013) A tale of caution and hope: From the frontlines. Retrieved from www.cft.org/news-publications/newsletters/california-teacher/september-october-2013/lessons-from-latin-america.html.
33 Eskelsen-García, L. (2015, May 19) Happiness is a post-standardized-test world. *Education Week*. Retrieved from http://blogs.edweek.org/edweek/rick_hess_straight_up/2015/05/happiness_post_standardized_test_world.html?r=2107712634&preview=1.
34 Canadian Teachers' Federation (2016) *International programs: Supporting teachers and public education worldwide*. Retrieved from www.ctf-fce.ca/en/Pages/International/Teacher-Opportunities.aspx.
35 Go to www.unite4education.org/.
36 Pritchett, L. (2013) *The rebirth of education: Schooling ain't learning*. Washington, DC: Center for Global Development.
37 Retrieved from www.un.org/millenniumgoals/poverty.shtml.
38 Go to www.quality4educationcampaign.org.
39 Go to www.tes.com/worldslargestlesson/.
40 Go to www.globalgoals.org/global-goals/quality-education.

References

Canadian Teachers' Federation (2016) *International programs: Supporting teachers and public education worldwide*. Retrieved from www.ctf-fce.ca/en/Pages/International/Teacher-Opportunities.aspx.

Delors, J., et al. (1996) *Learning: The treasure within*. Paris: UNESCO.

Draxler, A. (2010) The Delors commission and report. Geneva: Graduate Institute of International and Development Studies. Retrieved from www.norrag.org/es/publications/boletin-norrag/online-version/a-world-of-reports-a-critical-review-of-global-development-reports-with-an-angle-on-education-and-training/detail/the-delors-commission-and-report.html.

Eskelsen-García, L. (2015, May 19) Happiness is a post-standardized-test world. *Education Week*. Retrieved from http://blogs.edweek.org/edweek/rick_hess_straight_up/2015/05/happiness_post_standardized_test_world.html?r=2107712634&preview=1.

Faure, E., Herrera, F., Kaddoura, A., Lopes, H., Petrovsky, A., Rahnema, M., & Ward, F.C. (1972) *Learning to be: The world of education today and tomorrow*. Paris: UNESCO.

International Labor Office (2014) *Global employment trends 2014*. Geneva: International Labor Office.

International Labor Office (2015) *Making progress against child labor: Global estimates and trends, 2000–2012*. Geneva: International Labor Office.

Pechthalt, J. (2013) A tale of caution and hope: From the frontlines. Retrieved from www.cft.org/news-publications/newsletters/california-teacher/september-october-2013/lessons-from-latin-america.html.

Pritchett, L. (2013) *The rebirth of education: Schooling ain't learning.* Washington, DC: Center for Global Development.

Saxenian, A. (2006) *The new argonauts: Regional advantage in a global economy.* Cambridge, MA: Harvard University Press.

Skerrett, A. (2015) *Teaching transnational youth: Literacy and education in a changing world.* New York: Teachers College Press.

UNESCO (2015) *Rethinking education: Towards a global common good?* Paris: UNESCO.

UNESCO Institute for Statistics (2015) *A growing number of children and adolescents are out of school as aid fails to meet the mark.* Policy Paper 22/ Fact Sheet 31, p. 1. Retrieved from http://unesdoc.unesco.org/images/ 0023/002336/233610e.pdf.

UNICEF (2014, May 14) *Convention on the rights of the child: Advancing the CRC.* Retrieved from www.unicef.org/crc/index_protocols.html.

United Nations General Assembly (1990) Convention on the rights of the child. Retrieved from www.ohchr.org/en/professionalinterest/pages/crc. aspx.

6

THE EXISTENTIAL IMPERATIVE

THE ENDS OF EDUCATION

Let's review the first four new imperatives of educational change:

1 Check ideological biases and pursue a persistent *evidentiary imperative* with true impartiality.
2 Avoid imperial attitudes when setting policy and provide educators with tools so they can explore an *interpretive imperative* with increasing levels of sophistication.
3 Overcome the limitations of prescription and replace it with a genuine *professional imperative* for teachers, principals, and school staff.
4 Break through insularity, using the *global imperative* to enhance teaching and learning wherever you are.

To realize the first four new imperatives is a monumental challenge in itself, but it is still incomplete. During the years in which the old imperatives held sway, student well-being was so irrelevant to the achievement agenda it never figured into a single accountability matrix. The *ideological imperative* demanded choice and markets. The *imperial imperative* spread market ideologies to countries rich and poor. A *prescriptive imperative* made sure that practices emphasizing implementation with fidelity worked their way into every nook and cranny of classrooms and schools. The *insular imperative* prevented educators from learning from one another, and especially from systems and cultures that took a broader and deeper view of students' learning and development. While these old imperatives spread far and wide, what was happening to student well-being?

About one-fifth of students in the developed world suffer from depression, anxiety, or both. They need teachers who are sensitive to their plight and policies that acknowledge their challenges. Don't bother telling depressed students that if they study harder they'll find their way to a joyful future, because "measures of intelligence have, at most, a trivial relationship to happiness and usually no relation at all."[1] Formal schooling doesn't necessarily contribute to well-being because "when U.S. levels of education rose dramatically in the postwar years, they did not bring with them increasing levels of happiness and life satisfaction."[2] The opposite occurred. There has been a continuous upward trend in rates of depression and anxiety in the US from 1952 to the present.[3]

Are these US trends reflected in other countries? UNICEF provides reports on child well-being that are calculated using five indicators.[4] These are material well-being, health and safety, education, behavior and risks, and housing and the environment. The PISA scores of the OECD are factored into the rankings for educational well-being. These objective measures are combined with surveys where students are asked to report on their subjective well-being. Significantly, there is a strong correlation between the objective measures and students' self-assessment about their well-being.

UNICEF reports that European countries such as Holland, Norway, and Finland, lead the way in child well-being. These are nations with strong welfare states. The US, with a weaker welfare state, ranks at or near the bottom of the tables. It is clustered with Greece, Romania, and Spain at the lowest level of educational well-being. It is second from the bottom on relative child poverty rates, exceeded only by Romania.

The rise of depression and anxiety is correlated not only with chemical imbalances in the brain but also with feelings of isolation and lack of self-worth. The symptoms are psychological, but the causes often are social. Depression and anxiety are pervasive not only among the poor, but among all social classes in the US.[5] American youth report that they do not see themselves as having a choice among different ways to live but are curtailed by societal expectations

that value success and scorn failure. Because they have been social-
ized to accept these norms, they are locked in an endless battle for
status and prestige.

Happiness—what psychologists call "subjective well-being"—
should not be pursued directly. It is a byproduct of the quality of
one's relationships. To establish intimacy and trust, individuals need
to be able to risk vulnerability. They have to demonstrate to others
that they can be relied upon in good times and bad. These virtues
cannot be acquired rapidly. They need to be earned over time. They
require that students have opportunities to get to know themselves
and to overcome adversity so that they acquire a strong personal
identity.

Schools can play a part in either developing or neglecting students'
subjective well-being. They cannot do so, however, when they are
locked into an instrumental mindset that views students exclusively in
terms of their ability to produce a good return on society's investment
in them. Children and adolescents are not raw material to be ham-
mered into profits. They have their own interests that they want to
pursue and their own personalities to develop. Caring educators respect
and nourish this spirited independence. When adults treat children
only or mainly as human capital, adults lose their moral bearings.

So some reformers have advocated "personalized" or "customized"
learning in order to counterbalance the human capital approach.
These programs give students freedom to design their own learning
to go beyond being consumers of others' information to "prosumers"
who create their own knowledge. Some advocates of these approaches
exude a heady, almost utopian optimism with the range of new
instructional offerings available through new technologies in particular. They foresee futures in which students can learn what they
want, how they want, and when they want.

The "Teach to One" (formerly "School of One") in New York
City is a good example of personalized learning. Students using
computer software choose their own modality of mathematics curricula from "learning playlists" based on algorithms of their online
assessments. Students are not told only one way to learn mathematics, but have a variety of approaches to explore. "School of One"
reformers have shared numerous reports of positive results on their

home page. They have also acknowledged openly that one major study of their program thus far found "no statistically significant effects on student achievement—positive or negative—relevant to traditional mathematics instruction."[6]

Innovations in personalized learning like in the "School of One" are valuable. They give students choices that they have never had about their preferred ways to learn. We should not confuse such new individual freedoms and choices about learning modalities, however, with our responsibilities to provide students with a sense of meaning and belonging. When students have too many choices, they become overwhelmed. When the choices have high stakes, the fear of making the wrong choice can "even be said to tyrannize," according to Barry Schwarz.[7] While it seems counter-intuitive, the reality is that too many choices cause unhappiness.

Choice does not always provide avenues to depth in how we learn or who we are either. No one pretends that playlists of curricular offerings help students to find meaning in their lives. This has to occur on a different level altogether.

The shortcomings of the old imperatives have not gone unnoticed by a cottage industry of keynote speakers who have taken aim at recent reforms. These speakers have understood that reducing students to human capital will not lead to achievement with integrity. Their recommendations, unfortunately, have serious shortcomings of their own. The recommendations could make education more entertaining, but they can also lead it to become aligned with a consumer society that promotes immediate gratification as the solution to every problem. They avoid the very real injustices and environmental challenges that face our planet. If teachers and other educators follow their recommendations, they will produce students who are self-absorbed, believe that they have a right to do whatever they want whenever they want, and do not know how to compromise or settle differences with others.

Why Finding Your Passion Isn't Everything

Ken Robinson is an English educator who has written popular books on the importance of redesigning schools so that they become "the meeting place between natural aptitude and personal passion."[8] His runaway bestseller is entitled *The Element: How Finding Your Passion Changes Everything*.[9] In it, Robinson has described talented individuals—ballet dancer Gillian Lynne, cartoonist Matt Groening, Fleetwood Mac drummer Mick Fleetwood among them—who suffered in schools because their personalities were stifled. He does not blame individual teachers for their students' challenges. He questions the bureaucracies of schooling that disregard students' enthusiasms and that have become outdated in an age of instant digital communication.

How can educators help each student to find his or her Element? Robinson has a threefold strategy. First, "eliminate the existing hierarchy of subjects"[10] so that the arts and physical education are just as important as math and literacy. Second, "Schools should base their curriculum not on the idea of separate subjects, but on the much more fertile idea of disciplines" that allow students to learn "not just a set of information" but rather "a complex pattern of ideas, practical skills, and concepts."[11] Finally, "the curriculum should be personalized" in order to "take account of individual learning styles and talents."[12]

Robinson does not just describe these strategies in the abstract, but also depicts real schools in the throes of innovation. In the best instances, the test scores go up, but Robinson is mining for deeper gold. He seeks out evidence that students are set afire with passion to pursue their own freely chosen dreams.

It's an ambitious agenda. Robinson has understood that adolescents are at the stage of what Erik Erikson described as identity versus role confusion.[13] While adults might like to assign to children and teens a preferred identity, the young have a way of rebelling against authorities and asserting their own existential ways of being in the world. If adults are wise, Robinson argues, they will not block the young in this path to individuation but rather will engage with it. They will provide innovative curricula and responsive pedagogies that help the young to find their own freely chosen passions to pursue. It's a scenario in which real joy and moral purpose can be brought into schools.

Robinson is nonjudgmental about what passions students should develop. He is adamant about the role of education in crafting a life of dignity and beauty. Some of his ideas—like taking principles from organic farming and applying them to schools to engender "organic education"—exhibit the very creativity he wants everyone to possess.[14] The popular resonance to his message should send a wake-up call to all advocates of standardization everywhere.

The pursuit of one's passion has an intuitive appeal. Robinson has struck a chord. But there are three problems with his recommendations. The first is that Robinson is all about the joy individuals experience when they've found their passions. He doesn't mention the drudgery that is also part of the creative process. Beginning pianists practice scales. Learning a foreign language requires a lot of memorization. The indispensably hard parts of creativity that require dogged persistence have been left out.

A second problem is his idealization of the relationship between finding one's passion and developing a healthy pro-social attitude among students. In reality, creative geniuses can be anti-social or worse. The poet Ezra Pound adored Mussolini. The playwright George Bernard Shaw admired Hitler and Stalin. Nobel Prize winning author Jorge Luis Borges supported the military junta in Argentina.

Students are no different than people anywhere. They can develop passions for awful things as well as admirable ones. Educators shouldn't simply celebrate that their students have found their passions. They should have the wisdom to help to form and at times actively redirect those passions. This need not require authoritarianism. It can be done through tactful, caring dialogue with students from a position of genuine good will.

Third, Robinson assumes that once individuals find their passions, they will be static and fixed. Most passions, however, change over time. Many are fleeting, no matter how compelling they appear at any one moment. Just look at the duration of the average teenage romance! Adolescents have multiple, competing, and constantly shifting interests.

Educators should not believe that once their students find their passions, this will "change everything." Teachers should accept that teenagers, like everyone, have a mixture of passions. Some of these are good. Others are not. Jimi Hendrix, Janis Joplin, and Jim Morrison all had passions, but their life narratives do not find their way into Robinson's books. Their inabilities to master their passions destroyed them.

We should learn from these experiences and should encourage our students to develop their reason so that they can avoid similar fates. We need reason to be taught in schools so that students will develop into mature adults who understand that their passions will come and go throughout their lives. Indulging in one's passions can indeed be a source of great joy, but also of peril. If students can detach from their passions from time to time, they can bring greater balance and purpose to their lives.

Passion is sexy. Reason is not. There are no best-selling books spreading the message that "using your reason changes everything." But developing students' reason is a primary responsibility of schools, including those old-fashioned brick-and-mortar buildings practicing what Robinson describes as "industrial/academic education."[15]

Schools historically have taught students to develop habits of personal prudence and restraint that require short-term sacrifices for long-term gains. A long and distinguished body of academic research has shown that students who are able to delay gratification experience advantages over their peers. Their academic achievement is higher, they withstand stress better, and they are less likely to fall prey to alcoholism or other forms of substance abuse.[16]

Students who have learned to defer gratification have become skilled at using their reason to understand that immediate satisfaction of many of their cravings has negative long-term consequences. They have learned that they will be better off if instead of giving in to passions they learn to control their behavior. Such adjustment of behaviors is not innate, but it can be learned in school.

Robinson is right that schools have gone too far in the direction of standardization, testing, and prescription. He's also right that we need a major paradigm shift toward a more humanistic model of education. But to achieve this worthy goal, we'll have to learn how to balance passion with the uniquely human gift of reason.

The Entrepreneurial Ideal

Tony Wagner is a US educator who has built strong relationships between the worlds of education and business. Wagner's best-selling book, *The Global Achievement Gap*, argued that schools need to provide students with skills that are honed to "the new world of work."[17] CEOs whom Wagner interviewed wanted schools to prepare critical thinkers who would help their businesses to innovate to be more competitive. According to Wagner, "there is a convergence between the skills most needed for work in the global knowledge economy and those most needed to keep our democracy safe and vibrant."[18] His contention is that "corporations are increasingly being organized around a very different kind of authority and accountability structure—one that is less hierarchical and more reciprocal and relational."[19]

It's a provocative argument. Unfortunately, it bears no relationship to reality. In the same year that *The Global Achievement Gap* was published, the world entered the worst economic recession since the 1930s. Businesses fired employees by the thousands and cut their remaining employees' benefits to the bone. The pay of top CEOs soared and the decline of the middle and working classes accelerated. Recent investigative reporting by the *New York Times* into the practices of the most rapidly growing businesses, such as amazon.com, have revealed a nightmare of surveillance and control by top executives over their rank and file workers.[20] These are the stark realities of the business world today. They play no part in Wagner's light and bubbly narratives.

Wagner's interpretation of educational change is similar to Robinson's insofar as each caters to wish fulfillment. If only we could redesign schools so that students could find their "Element," all would be well. If only we could promote innovative and entrepreneurial skills, all students would thrive. The needs of businesses and democracies are identical. Collective action is anachronistic. Delayed gratification is a bore. Principled conflict is passé.

While this book was being written, the government in Syria was bombing its own citizens. Videos documenting racial profiling and police brutality toward African-Americans shocked (or at least, *should* have shocked) the national conscience in the US. If current environmental trends continue vast stretches of the world's deltas that have sustained indigenous cultures since time immemorial will be submerged under water in coming decades. Income inequality is rising within and among nations.

These are the epochal challenges of our time. A rising generation did not choose these problems, but that is irrelevant. Educators have the responsibility to teach their students disagreeable truths about the world they are inheriting. This requires skills in critical thinking, evidence gathering, synthesis, and argumentation.

Educators should be friends to the business community, not flatterers. The profession has its own norms and traditions. It has nurtured these over centuries. They have improved the human condition. Now is not the time for wavering off course.

Getting to the Heart of the Matter

Education has to be about more than indulging passions and more than drawing superficial comparisons between the attitudes adapted to run a business and those necessary for democratic citizenship. Education, from the Latin "*educare*," usually is defined in terms of leading forth or drawing out, but one also should note that it has the word "care" within it. This takes us into the heart of the matter.

Consider three cases of students and teachers in the midst of change. The first case comes from a suburban high school in which I was using the "tuning protocol" developed by the Coalition of Essential Schools.[21] The tuning protocol is a tool that enables educators to discuss a difficult situation with which they need collegial support. It takes educators through a clearly developed sequence of case presentation, factual questions, group deliberation, and collective evaluation. It is popular because it allows educators to surface a large amount of information rapidly in a shared quest for practical solutions.

The case in the suburban high school related to a student with a learning disability whose mother had emailed his English teacher 135 times in the school year to check in about assignments, ask about his progress, or to complain about a grade. The English teacher was exasperated beyond belief—especially because the boy's Individualized Education Plan called for him to take on responsibility for his own learning. The colleagues pooled their information to organize what became a successful conference with the teacher, the mother, and the boy that restored the theme of self-regulation to the boy's Individualized Education Plan.

The second case, also using the tuning protocol, surfaced when I was leading a "Mindful Teacher" seminar for urban teachers several years ago along with teacher leader Elizabeth MacDonald.[22] In this case a combined Kindergarten-Grade 1 teacher had observed that a boy in her class was alternately hyperactive or listless on different days of the week. She was worried that his mother might be giving him Ritalin, which is available as a street drug in poorer communities, and is sometimes given to children when parents' nerves are frayed by the stressors they confront on a daily basis. The teacher recognized that she had no evidence about this one way or the other. She then discussed the issue with the school nurse and the principal, neither of whom was helpful. She was unclear about how to proceed and turned to her colleagues in the seminar for advice.

Teachers in the "Mindful Teacher" seminar were helpful with this teacher in discussing the complex issues that confront teachers when endeavoring to assist parents in impoverished communities. While it is easy to blame parents for ways that they raise and manage their children, many are coping with situations that are extraordinarily complicated given their minimal financial resources. The teachers were impressed with the degree of dedication shown by the presenting teacher, and they let the teacher know that many of them had struggled with similar cases in the past. They advised their younger colleague on ways that she could speak with the mother to let her know what she was observing about the boy's behavior and the gravity of the situation. While a difficult conversation with the mother ensued, it ultimately was successful. The boy's subsequent ability to learn improved.

The third case relates to a middle school social studies teacher in the US. In this case, an educator was exasperated by a student that was often truant. When the student did show up he was belligerent, intimidating not only his classmates but also the teacher. Discussion of the case in a professional learning community revealed that both of the parents of the student were known in the community to be methamphetamine users and dealers. The family's economic basis was unstable, the boy's older brother had already had multiple run-ins with law enforcement officers, and the parents were expecting another child. Already fully challenged by other students with few future economic prospects in their community, the teacher worried that he was losing any hope of engaging the boy.

At one point in the discussion, the presenting teacher whispered, "I've had my idealism beaten out of me." Colleagues recognized the frustration. They jumped in with suggestions of ways to respond. One teacher proposed finding something that could motivate the student to come to school. Since the parents would not come to school, one teacher proposed meeting with the parents in a neutral setting close to their home, so that the teacher could share his concern. A third teacher asked if the student was involved in any extracurricular activities that could help him to view school as a positive environment.

Cases such as these indicate that when teachers have opportunities to share problems with one another and to solve them without judgment or evaluation from those higher up in the school hierarchy that they can do so. At the end of the second case discussed above, the presenting teacher commented "I can't believe I just got so many good practical ideas, and we did all of this in less than an hour to solve a problem I've been struggling with all year." She was right about the many suggestions generated in the previous hour, but she was wrong insofar as it took five years of prior work to create the relational trust that enabled her to present her case in the first place. Without trust, teachers will not share vulnerabilities and they will not seek help for fear of appearing incompetent.

These cases point us toward a different understanding of education that engages the whole teacher and the whole student. They all concerned educators who were stretched to the breaking point as they struggled to assist students in need. In the first case a mother was intrusive, and in the second a mother was overburdened. In the third, the parents were criminals. Yet educators alone have been held accountable for student achievement. At such times, voices crack in frustration. Tears are fought back against. Colleagues who scarcely know each other in other settings share similar experiences and test out potential solutions.

Some of the issues teachers surface afford easy resolutions, but others will not. In situations of concentrated poverty, the school cannot be a panacea for all of the social problems that lie beyond its boundaries. The school can, however, be a place in which educators and their students bring their whole selves to encounter one another with dignity and respect.

The Quest for Meaning and Purpose

In Reggio Emilia, Italy, educators observe young children's interests carefully and use them as points of departure for curriculum development. Respecting the "hundred languages of children" or the many ways that children have of expressing themselves, educators design the school environment to maximize children's interests in individual subject matter exploration and group work.[23] Parents, along with teachers, are intimately involved with the teachers in shaping the curriculum, identifying topics that are important to them and their communities. This is education for student voice at a very young age, with developmental possibilities that have inspired teachers the world over.

In a rural community in the Pacific Northwest of the US, students and their educators observe an exodus of the young people for the cities as soon as they graduate from high school. With few job prospects in the immediate area, they make films as part of their English and social studies classes to promote attachment to and advocacy for their community. Even if graduates have to leave for economic reasons, their teachers want them to continue to feel a connection to their old hometown.[24]

In the provincial capital city of Edmonton in Alberta, Canada, students are upset to learn that their schools are bracing for massive funding cuts. They organize themselves using social media, with the assistance of their educators. When the cuts are approved regardless, the students evaluate what had happened and agitate for the right to elect a student to the city school board. This time they prevail, so that in the future they will have greater influence about the future of education in Edmonton.[25]

In non-elite schools in Beijing, China, educators decide not to focus on examinations and instead to retrieve indigenous knowledge by incorporating Confucian and ethnic minority heritages into the curriculum.[26] They create an ethnic museum for their students and work with mosques to help students learn about China's Muslim minority culture. At the same time, they adapt elements of western pedagogies that allow more student choice than is permitted in the competitive elite schools. Parents in the community are delighted to find that their children are excited about their education, and as a consequence, the schools are oversubscribed.

Educators everywhere know that they and their students want to find meaning and purpose in their lives. They know that if the quest for meaning can be linked with the academic dimensions of schools that they will have made major contributions to their students' understanding and to their well-being.

Of all of the new imperatives in this book, the *existential imperative* to help students find meaning in their lives matters the most to me. This is for autobiographical reasons. My first elementary school was administered by the US Department of Defense on Via Manzoni in Naples, Italy, where I attended grades 1–4. Italians are famous for their love of children, and Americans were idolized in Naples as liberators who drove out the German occupiers during World War II. Unsurprisingly, I have only positive memories of this time. Youthful US President John Kennedy visited Naples in the summer of 1963, and optimism abounded. Everything seemed possible.

Just four years later, in 1969, the idyllic world that I knew as a child was shattered forever. President Kennedy, his brother Bobby, and Martin Luther King, Jr. had all been assassinated, extinguishing hopes for inspiring leadership in the US. My father, who had been so proud and happy in Naples, was caught up in the war in Vietnam. I was delivering the *Washington Evening Star* at the time and there was no hiding from the headlines. The polarization in my high school was at fever pitch, with some students wearing black armbands to protest the war and others wearing red, white, and blue ones to support it.

I found refuge at the time in the English Department at my high school. Our teachers exposed us to literature such as Aeschylus' *Oedipus Rex*, Thomas Mann's *Death in Venice*, and Richard Wright's *Native Son*. One of my teachers allowed me to do an independent study of Herman Melville's *Moby Dick*, which changed my life forever. More than four decades later, I still get together with my three best friends from high school every year in a cabin in West Virginia. One of them assembles in advance a selection of poetry that we pore over beside the comforting glow of a wood stove in the evenings.

In a just world, there would be some way to let my teachers know just how precious was the gift that they passed on to me. They exposed me to literature that let me know that I was not the first or only person to experience a turbulent adolescence. They exposed me to authors who wrote about life in ancient Greece, cholera-infected Venice, and the South Side of Chicago in such vivid and powerful ways that I became addicted to books and insatiably curious about the world at large.

If you're lucky to have teachers like I had, it becomes impossible to reduce education to the mere acquisition of academic content knowledge or the computational skills needed to pass tests. You've learned that education, when properly encountered, can provide students with aspirations for a life of meaning, beauty, and purpose. You've learned that education can awaken the conscience, teach compassion, and spark a lifelong dedication to contributing to a better world.

Students want to believe that educators are invested in them. "Don't give up on us," one high school student from Canada pleaded in a report. "Even though we aren't always easy and we know your jobs are really hard, please don't give up on us!" This isn't a request for better tutoring or advising. It is a plea for a leap of faith that even the most oppositional and recalcitrant of student wants to belong and wants to understand. These are not only means to something else. These are the ends of education.

The old *instrumental imperative* will not help students to address the deeper and more demanding facets of teaching and learning. Nor will messages that pander to students' fleeting passions or their entrepreneurial ambitions without awakening them to the harsh realities of an unjust world. Educators must be forthright with students. This is not optional. It is an *existential imperative*. It leads us to a better understanding of our professional obligations for achievement with integrity.

Notes

1 Lane, R.E. (2000) *The loss of happiness in market democracies*. New Haven, CT: Yale University Press, p. 45.

2 Lane, *The loss of happiness*, p. 45.
3 Wilkinson, R., & Pickett, K. (2009) *The spirit level: Why greater equality makes societies stronger*. New York: Bloomsbury.
4 Adamson, P. (2013) *Child well-being in rich countries: A comparative overview*. Florence: UNICEF Office of Research—Innocenti. Mortorano, B., Natali, L., Neubourg, C., & Bradshaw, J. (2013) *Child well-being in advanced economies in the late 2000s*. Florence: UNICEF Office of Research—Innocenti.
5 Luthar, S.S. (2003) The culture of affluence: Psychological costs of material wealth. *Child Development* 74(6), 1581–1593.
6 Retrieved from http://izonenyc.org/initiatives/school-of-one/.
7 Schwartz, B. (2004) *The paradox of choice: Why more is less*. New York: Harper Perennial, p. 2.
8 Robinson, K. (2001) *Out of our minds: Learning to be creative*. Chichester: Capstone; (2009) *The element: How finding your passion changes everything*. New York: Penguin; (2013) *Finding your element: How to discover your talents and passions and transform your life*. New York: Penguin; (2015) *Creative schools: The grassroots revolution that's transforming education*. New York: Viking. The quote is from Robinson, *The element*, p. 21.
9 Robinson, *The element*.
10 Robinson, *The element*, p. 247.
11 Robinson, *The element*, p. 248.
12 Robinson, *The element*, p. 248.
13 Erikson, E. (1968) *Identity: Youth and crisis*. New York: Norton.
14 Robinson, *Creative schools*, pp. 41–45.
15 Robinson, *Out of our minds*, p. 109.
16 See Roberts, P. (2014) *The impulse society: America in the age of instant gratification*. New York: Bloomsbury.
17 Wagner, T. (2008) *The global achievement gap*. New York: Basic Books, p. 1.
18 Wagner, *The global achievement gap*, p. 28.
19 Wagner, *The global achievement gap*, p. 28.
20 Kantor, J., & Streitfeld, D. (2015, August 15) Inside Amazon: Wrestling big ideas in a bruising workplace. *New York Times*. Retrieved from www.nytimes.com/2015/08/16/technology/inside-amazon-wrestling-big-ideas-in-a-bruising-workplace.html?_r=0.
21 McDonald, J.P., Mohr, N., Dichter, A., & McDonald, E.C. (2003) *The power of protocols: An educator's guide to better practice*. New York: Teachers College Press.
22 Shirley, D., & MacDonald, E. (2016) *The mindful teacher*. New York: Teachers College Press.
23 Edwards, C., Gandini, L., & Forman, G. (Eds.) (1998) *The hundred languages of children: The Reggio Emilia approach—advanced reflections*. Westwood, CT: Ablex.
24 I would like to thank my colleagues at the Northwest Rural Innovations and Student Engagement (RISE) of Education Northwest for welcoming Andy Hargreaves, Michael O'Connor, and me to their remote rural communities in February 2015. Go to http://educationnorthwest.org/news/road-nw-rise-promoting-student-engagement-rural-schools.
25 Shirley, D. (2015) *Student voice: A catalyst for educational change*. ICSEI Monograph Series: Issue 7. Springwood, Australia: International Congress for School Effectivenesss and Improvement.
26 Tan, C. (2016) Teacher agency and school curriculum in China's non-elite schools. *Journal of Educational Change*. Retrieved from http://link.springer.com/journal/10833#page-1.

References

Adamson, P. (2013) *Child well-being in rich countries: A comparative overview*. Florence: UNICEF Office of Research—Innocenti.

Edwards, C., Gandini, L., & Forman, G. (Eds.) (1998) *The hundred languages of children: The Reggio Emilia approach—advanced reflections*. Westwood, CT: Ablex.

Erikson, E. (1968) *Identity: Youth and crisis*. New York: Norton.

Kantor, J., & Streitfeld, D. (2015, August 15) Inside Amazon: Wrestling big ideas in a bruising workplace. *New York Times*. Retrieved from www.nytimes.com/2015/08/16/technology/inside-amazon-wrestling-big-ideas-in-a-bruising-workplace.html?_r=0.

Lane, R.E. (2000) *The loss of happiness in market democracies*. New Haven, CT: Yale University Press.

Luthar, S.S. (2003) The culture of affluence: Psychological costs of material wealth. *Child Development* 74(6), 1581–1593.

McDonald, J.P., Mohr, N., Dichter, A., & McDonald, E.C. (2003) *The power of protocols: An educator's guide to better practice*. New York: Teachers College Press.

Mortorano, B., Natali, L., Neubourg, C., & Bradshaw, J. (2013) *Child well-being in advanced economies in the late 2000s*. Florence: UNICEF Office of Research—Innocenti.

Roberts, P. (2014) *The impulse society: America in the age of instant gratification*. New York: Bloomsbury.

Robinson, K. (2001) *Out of our minds: Learning to be creative*. Chichester: Capstone.

Robinson, K. (2009) *The element: How finding your passion changes everything*. New York: Penguin.

Robinson, K. (2013) *Finding your element: How to discover your talents and passions and transform your life*. New York: Penguin.

Robinson, K. (2015) *Creative schools: The grassroots revolution that's transforming education*. New York: Viking.

Schwartz, B. (2004) *The paradox of choice: Why more is less*. New York: Harper Perennial.

Shirley, D. (2015) *Student voice: A catalyst for educational change*. ICSEI Monograph Series: Issue 7. Springwood, Australia: International Congress for School Effectivenesss and Improvement.

Shirley, D., & MacDonald, E. (2016) *The mindful teacher*. New York: Teachers College Press.

Tan, C. (2016) Teacher agency and school curriculum in China's non-elite schools. *Journal of Educational Change*. Retrieved from http://link.springer.com/journal/10833#page-1.

Wagner, T. (2008) *The global achievement gap*. New York: Basic Books.

Wilkinson, R., & Pickett, K. (2009) *The spirit level: Why greater equality makes societies stronger*. New York: Bloomsbury.

7

ACHIEVEMENT WITH INTEGRITY

Chapter 1 of this book delineated four possible relationships between achievement and integrity:

1   low achievement, low integrity;
2   low achievement, high integrity;
3   high achievement, low integrity; and
4   high achievement, high integrity.

Throughout this volume, I have argued that five old imperatives of educational change working together as an ensemble led to testing with fidelity, whereas we need to be aspiring for achievement with integrity. To reach that goal, we need new imperatives of educational change. These will unite a fresh study of the available evidence, skills in the arts of interpretation, and a renewed understanding of the teaching profession. These will bring together the aspirations of humanity as a whole and the needs of the individual for meaning and purpose.

The five new imperatives are not only related to one another—they are dependent upon each other. It won't help to study evidence intensely in a context of prescribed professionalism. Little will be gained by promoting the existential imperative in the absence of a shared commitment to uplifting the conditions of all students, and especially those who are denied access to formal schooling. Piecemeal gains may occur but we should be in pursuit of larger goals that required a unified approach.

We all should endeavor as best we can to live out lives of personal integrity. Insofar as we are able to do so, we improve the human condition. Placing too much of the onus for integrity on individuals, as has occurred in the school cheating scandals in the US, however, is too easy. None of those educators entered the profession with the intention of cheating children. Institutions and the habitual ways of being they produce are more powerful than isolated individuals in promoting or eroding integrity. Personal integrity is essential but in the real world must be buttressed with collective responsibility. To promote the integrity of the profession, and not just individuals, let's revisit key ideas of this book to explore how different parts of them fit together.

The Evidentiary and Interpretive Imperatives

Just as policy makers need to study the evidence of stagnant or declining student achievement results in England, Sweden, and the US, so do educators at the classroom, school, or district level need to engage with evidence. This should include standardized examinations but not be limited to them. The evidence should not be fetishized, but it should not be ignored either.

The current opportunity for educators who seek to enact achievement with integrity is to get better with how we study and make use of evidence. Research from around the world indicates that a long-term, collective approach is essential.[1] Providing teachers with one-off workshops, or leaving them to puzzle over data on their own has not worked. Neither has reactive leadership that fails to mediate the data with a critical stance regarding its very real limitations.

Instead, educators need to decide how to go about studying student learning in ways that are sensitive to their own cultures. In Asia, methods of collaborative lesson study that first began in Japan have become popular throughout the region. These are being adapted by educators who are giving lesson study their own particular emphases in response to local circumstances.[2] In Europe, a framework of "didactic analysis" created by Wolfgang Klafki helps educators to ensure that the curriculum connects to the current lives and future needs of students.[3] In Latin America, Paolo Freire's pedagogy of "problem-posing" education has been infused into teacher education and professional development offerings.[4] Such approaches provide a rich fund of knowledge that should be open to all teachers.

Lesson study, didactic analysis, and problem-posing education will endure regardless of shifting policy winds because they get to the heart of teaching and learning. They respect the dignity of educators' quests to better understand and uplift their students' learning. The complexity of teaching generates countless questions for educators that call out for shared deliberation.

Teachers have responded with enthusiasm to the idea of "mindful teaching" because it extends to them an *interpretive imperative* to think about how they teach. This includes their ability to modify their pedagogies, to make informed curricular choices, and to select assessments that measure their students' learning. One recent OECD study found that contrary to what is sometimes espoused, teachers want to try out new ideas.[5] They want time and space to reflect on what they are learning so that their professional judgment is engaged and their knowledge of student learning is deepened.

It isn't so much that data-driven approaches have been wrong in the past. They played a helpful role in moving the profession beyond ambiguity and license. But the pendulum swung too far. Data can identify problems, but cannot dictate solutions. This explains why the *interpretive imperative* is so important. Between policy makers and the students stand not just compliant line managers but professionals who are able to make good judgments. They should help our students to thrive in forms of artistic excellence, scientific creativity, and mathematical abstraction that reach beyond current evaluation systems.

What could this mean for your professional life? Work with your colleagues to get better at studying evidence, while also allowing free play for diverse interpretations of the data. Encourage rigorous analysis of the numbers, but also be attuned to the everyday interactions of our students with one another, as these will reveal aspects of their personalities that influence their learning and that the tests could never uncover. Practice humility, as there always so many aspects of our students that elude us.

The Professional Imperative

Each new imperative is at educators' disposal to raise questions and to stimulate professional conversations. Each can be deployed in face-to-face conversations and activated by groups and in schools. Each can help you and your colleagues as references to consider in your quest to attain high levels of student achievement accompanied by deep professional integrity. You and your students deserve no less.

How do we know that each imperative has a solid foundation in current research? One way is to conduct fact checking. For example, do the findings presented in Chapter 4 on the *professional imperative* fit into broader research on educational change?

The answer is affirmative. Each of the cases presented in Chapter 4 is congruent with well-established research and corresponding professional frameworks. Singapore's demonstration of a solid professional knowledge base corresponds to the human capital strand of professional capital and the TALIS criteria. The LCP in Mexico provides a vivid illustration of social capital as expressed through peer learning networks. Mindful teaching in Arizona illuminates the value of decisional capital or professional autonomy, as conveyed by the professional capital and TALIS frameworks respectively. Not one of these cases exemplify the now discredited *prescriptive imperative* that held sway in too many jurisdictions for too many years.

Critical questions should of course be asked of the evidence supporting the professional imperative. To take tutorial relations in Mexican middle schools as an example, do we really know that it is worthwhile for teachers to teach students on ways to tutor each other? In John Hattie's meta-analysis (2009) of peer tutoring in *Invisible Learning*, he found that "The overall effects of the use of peers as co-teachers (of themselves and of others) in classes is [*sic*], overall, quite powerful."[6] Furthermore, among "the peer interventions that were more student controlled ... the effects were greater than when these were primarily controlled by the teacher."[7]

Hattie's analysis does not mean that peer tutoring always is successful. The best ideas can be implemented poorly, and they sometimes are. It does mean that the weight of the evidence, when aggregated, supports peer tutoring as an effective way to improve learning.

If peer learning works for students, do we really know that peer learning networks among educators are so beneficial? Collegial relationships can be superficial and distracting, after all. Couldn't the popularity of professional learning communities be overstated?

That educators, like students, need opportunities to learn from one another is indeed a common research finding.[8] Virtually every narrative of a troubled school or district that turned around has emphasized the collective nature of the endeavor. Impoverished Union City in New Jersey in the US defied expectations and uplifted performance by spreading norms of collegiality, offering high quality mentoring for all beginning teachers, and providing patient and hands-on coaching for struggling mid-career teachers.[9] Wakefield City High School in England climbed to the top of the rankings by emphasizing that not just "Every Child Matters" but also "Every Person Matters."[10] In the words of Barbara Kellerman, it appears as if we are experiencing "the end of leadership," when leadership is understood primarily as the attributes of an individual.[11]

Still, in the rush to push professional learning communities into every nook and cranny of schools, cautionary notes from scholars have been ignored. A quarter of a century ago Judith Warren Little warned, "Teachers are now being pressed, invited, and cajoled into ventures in 'collaboration,' but the organization of their daily work often gives them scant reason for doing so."[12] Andy Hargreaves argued that "contrived collegiality" could lead to the ostracism of independent spirits while being used as a ruse to get teachers to comply with the dictates of their principals or superintendents.[13] Similarly, Betty Achinstein contended that the very language of "teacher community" revealed a failure to appreciate "the differences within and between communities, thus minimizing issues of diversity."[14] Achinstein observed that it was essential for school leaders who want to create a more inclusive profession to anticipate conflict and to learn to work with it. Even then there are no guarantees, as some conflict-averse educators who dislike the acrimonious tone that can accompany argumentation may choose to leave their schools or the profession altogether.

Fortunately, we've learned a great deal about collegiality since these critical accounts.[15] Warren Little's critique that the contours of teachers' work make collegiality unlikely is being addressed by the creation of new roles for educators that enable them to stay in the classroom as teachers while receiving release time to mentor others, develop new curricular projects and engage with the community.[16] Hargreaves' criticisms of "contrived collegiality" remain valid in some settings, but in general teachers' reluctance to participate in professional learning communities can be addressed when skillful "network brokers" approach them as individuals and assure them that their challenges will be addressed in supportive ways by their colleagues.[17]

Achinstein's criticisms focused on the ways in which the language of "teacher community" could suppress diverse opinions. Educators need to be attentive to the ways in which language can exclude dissidents. Still, this legitimate concern should not be misconstrued. It is not true that the creation of shared values among diverse groups is impossible. If this were true we could have no International Convention on the Rights of the Child. We could have no Sustainable Development Goals. Defying skeptics, 195 nations signed on to the Paris Climate Agreement in December 2015 to lower their greenhouse gas emissions. If almost all of the diverse nations around the world can come together to agree upon such shared aims, cannot educators do the same within the far more manageable space of the school?

As a profession, we require environments in which we can share our frustrations about our work with each other—about a curriculum we chose that didn't work out, about a time we lost our patience with a misbehaving child, or about a parent–teacher conference that went badly. Teaching is a sensitive craft. It requires more than technical skills because it has to engage the emotions if it is to rouse the minds of students to peak engagement. It is time to create a new and more expansive *professional imperative* in our schools. It also is time to provide the skillful leadership and additional supports in our schools so that this new imperative can be brought to full fruition.

The Global and Existential Imperatives

In the final weeks of writing this book the media have been filled with stories about thousands of refugees streaming into Europe seeking asylum. Images of the best and worst of Europe have been

projected around the world, including cheering welcoming commit-
tees on the one hand and the gassing of desperate refugees, including
children, on the other. Germany has led the way in its hospitality,
welcoming over 325,000 refugee children into its public schools in
2015. Who knows what the future will hold for these displaced
peoples?

At the same time, nations continue to struggle to provide minimal
levels of equity for their own citizens. In the United States, racial
injustice doggedly persists in some areas, in spite of progress in
others. Class inequities have worsened. The country that once
boasted a proud middle class that led the world with high rates of
social mobility has cratered in the center. The consequences for children, both at home and at school, have been dire.[18]

Now, more than ever, we need education for "learning to be
together," as the UNESCO reports on education have so patiently
and persistently contended for decades now. We witness with heart-
breaking regularity a world calling out for direct action to rectify
injustices in our localities, our nations, and at a global level. But can
educators unite across our diverse jurisdictions from around the
world? Can we activate ourselves in ways that do not replicate past
patterns of domination mixed with charity so that we can expand our
potential to address the epochal challenges of our time?

We can indeed do this, at least in part by reinvigorating our dedication to the public realm and to public schools. The rhetoric of
marketplace advocates of reform has fallen flat because they simply
have not been able to match the levels of achievement of traditional
public schools. When Christopher and Sarah Lubienski set out to
compare the math results of private and public schools in the US,
they expected to see stronger results in the former, as marketplace
advocates would predict.[19] Instead, the public schools trounced the
private schools in the National Assessment of Education Progress
(NAEP) results. What happened?

The Lubienskis found that the alleged strength of the private
schools—their independence—was culpable for their poorer results.
Teachers in private schools, it seems, enjoy an expansive sense of academic freedom untethered to collective responsibility. The fact that
parents are paying tuition, often at very high rates, seems to be an

explicit register of their superiority to the public schools. Many of the reform waves of recent years consequently have passed them by altogether.

"Public schools," on the other hand, "are enjoying an advantage in academic effectiveness because they are aligned with a more professional model of teaching and learning."[20] NAEP standards are aligned with those established by the National Council of Teachers of Mathematics in the 1980s. The standards of this professional association, in turn, were informed by new insights from the learning sciences that focus on mathematics as cognition. The pedagogical and curricular reforms that have ensued "have been adopted with greater enthusiasm in the public school sector, often at the technocratic direction of those centralized bureaucracies so despised by market theory."[21]

Markets will continue to play important roles in education. In open and free societies, parents should always have the option to raise their children in schools that accommodate their particular faith traditions. We should not, however, expect markets to raise the performance of whole systems. To "learn to live together" we need collaborative models that do not pit us against one another. We need a profession that recognizes the dynamic and incremental nature of teaching and learning, and we need professional associations to help us to activate that knowledge.

In so many schools, teachers are overwhelmed with trying to master the day-to-day demands of meeting curricular standards, pushing up standardized test results, and attending prescribed professional development workshops. Who can blame them? There are so many pressures that if we step outside of the classroom to see what else might be going on we could lose precious traction. It is easier to stay within the carefully circumscribed paths others have set out for us.

Addressing the *global imperative* may only appeal to those restless spirits who are willing to go along with any number of government initiatives and policies, but just not all of them. This is a new imperative for those who don't just want to accommodate displaced peoples, but actually want to learn to be together with them. This is an imperative for those who want to do all that we can to ensure that

Mahbubani's "great convergence" is optimized, not just for one side or the other, but on behalf of everyone from host and sending countries alike. So much hangs in the balance with regard to our fragile futures. Only if we address our challenges collectively will we truly harmonize achievement with integrity.

What could this mean for you in your school or system? We can all be on the look-out for ways to expand our students' awareness beyond the limitations of our local settings. We can make sure that foreign language offerings are diverse and that we pay attention to equity in our classes and in our communities. At times we can raise our voices on behalf of those students without advocates at home or those without command of the language of the majority. Our curriculum should reflect the diversity of our students and should be projected toward the emerging world that so rapidly is replacing the old.

The Existential Imperative

European existentialists have been associated with the most troubling dimensions of human existence. Soren Kierkegaard wrote essays with titles like "Fear and Trembling" and "The Sickness unto Death."[22] Jean-Paul Sartre's novel *Nausea* portrayed a man who found he had been living in a state of inauthenticity by writing a biography, instead of facing up to his own situation.[23] In *The Ethics of Ambiguity* Simone de Beauvoir berated the so-called "serious man" who sought to lose his identity in that of a social movement or political party.[24]

There are other, more hopeful aspects of existentialism. For German émigré Erich Fromm, an existential stance meant going beyond the pressures of market societies "to have" and instead to focus on the potential "to be."[25] Abraham Maslow believed that we can capitalize even on traumatic experiences to become "self-actualizing" through proper cultivation of our interior lives.[26] Rollo May found a persistent anxiety to run through modern life with all of its competitive pressures, but argued that the human capacity to love would prevail.[27]

Existentialism is no longer as popular as it once was, but the quest for meaning remains as salient as ever. Meaning cannot be forced onto individuals. It must be earned from within. Yet even here educators can play a role.

We need educators who understand the "dignity of pedagogy" as a subtle spiritual act.[28] Good pedagogy requires tact and restraint so that the educator creates time and space for students to engender their own ideas and questions about the curriculum. Education is about knowledge transmission and acquisition, but it can also be the practice of freedom if educators are willing to create activities in their own classroom that enable students to wonder, to try out new ideas, and to revise them.

Education as an *existential imperative* can be developed from a variety of religious and secular perspectives. For Jewish theologian Martin Buber, educators had a responsibility to create environments of what he called "I-Thou" vertical depth that would go beyond the "I-It" world of instrumental horizontality.[29] Jesuit educational thought emphasizes the careful formation of the young to become "men and women for others" with devotion to the common good.[30] In Islamic philosophies, educators are called to model for the young ways in which to overcome selfish impulses in service to the larger community.[31] Buddhist philosophies of education call for teachers to practice the emptying out of ego as part of the path to enlightenment.[32] These traditions provide resources for all of us regardless of our personal backgrounds. Increasingly, they are combined into a diversity of forms in what has been called "postmodern spirituality."[33]

One hundred years ago this year, John Dewey published *Democracy and Education*, a *magnum opus* for all of those concerned with creating an optimal relationship between schools and society.[34] Without reference to explicit religious language, Dewey charted out a path that could uphold the critical thinking of the individual, ensure that education contributes to social progress, and do so in a non-ideological, pragmatic way. Dewey understood that education is both a means and an end, both an individual and a social matter. His theories of education have had an enormous impact globally and especially in East Asia, where a Dewey renaissance is underway today.

All of those approaches invite educators to go far beyond education as a mechanistic construct that is defined by the economic vagaries of the day. In each of them the educator needs to work extensively on developing an inner frame of mind that brings to light a subtle and sacred dimension of the pedagogical encounter. It does not matter if educators falter. None of us are perfect. What matters is that we engage in the struggle and persist over time.

The Promise of the Present Moment

Educators are standing on the brink of an enormous precipice today. The profession has higher academic content standards and more assessment data than ever. While inequities persist, the "great convergence" is providing us with opportunities to overcome the barriers to greater cooperation and toward greater social harmony and freedom. We are inheritors of noble intellectual traditions and an international canon of philosophies and religions that we can draw on as we lead our profession in the years ahead.

The old imperatives of change have been shaken to their core. When the president of the US takes time away from managing the crisis in the Middle East to issue a public statement on the excesses of testing in public schools, the tide has turned. When student protestors in Chile force a reversal of the privatization of schools, change is imminent. When the Minister of Education in Sweden puts together a high-level commission of teachers' unions, educational researchers, and concerned citizens to stop the nation's precipitous fall in the PISA results, the old imperatives are exhausted.

Educators now are being given new opportunities to shape the future of our profession. Will we have the courage to step up and to take charge? Will we develop collective professional integrity in which educators hold one another to the highest standards? How the profession reacts or leads will speak volumes about who we are and what we stand for. Our students and the public will be watching.

This book has been organized around imperatives. The choice of term may be disconcerting to those who privilege choice. But choice should not be its own end. It should serve higher purposes.

Choice is easy. Imperatives are hard. The arguments presented in this book will not persuade those who want to evade the epochal challenges of our time. The point of view presented here can only be persuasive if it speaks to the personal and professional quest of educators for meaning and purpose wherever they might be.

In the end, it is not possible *not* to have a legacy. Not deciding what kind of legacy we will leave is to cheat our students and to betray ourselves. We know what we need to do in schools and society: We need to attain achievement with integrity. Whether or not we leave this legacy to future generations—that will be all that matters in the end.

Notes

1 Datnow, A., & Hubbard, L. (2016) Teacher capacity for and beliefs about data-driven decision making: A literature review of international research. *Journal of Educational Change* 17(1), 7–28. See also Datnow, A., & Park, V. (2014) *Data-driven leadership*. San Francisco: Jossey-Bass.

2 Saito, E., Khong, T.D.H., & Tsukui, A. (2012) Why is school reform sustained even after a project? A case study of Bac Giang Province, Vietnam. *Journal of Educational Change* 13(2), 259–287.

3 Meyer, M.A., & Meyer, H. (2007) *Wolfgang Klafki: Eine Didaktik für das 21. Jahrhundert?* [Wolfgang Klafki: A didactic for the 21st century?]. Weinheim: Beltz Verlag.

4 O'Cadiz, M., Wong, P.L., & Torres, C.A. (1998) *Education and democracy: Paolo Freire, social movements, and educational reform in São Paolo*. Boulder, CO: Westview.

5 OECD (2014) *Measuring innovation in education: A new perspective*. Paris: OECD.

6 Hattie, J. (2009) *Visible learning: A synthesis of 800 meta-analyses relating to achievement*. New York: Routledge, p. 186.

7 Hattie, *Visible learning*, p. 187.

8 Bryk, A.S., Gomez, L.M., Grunow, A., & LeMahieu, P.G. (2015) *Learning to improve: How America's schools can get better at getting better*. Cambridge, MA: Harvard Education Press.

9 Kirp, D.L. (2013) *Improbable scholars: The rebirth of a great American school system and a strategy for America's schools*. New York: Oxford University Press.

10 Yessup, A. (2013) Making sure every person matters. In: Crossley, D. (Ed.) *Sustainable school transformation: An inside-out school led approach*. London: Bloomsbury, pp. 253–276.

11 Kellerman, B. (2012) *The end of leadership*. New York: Harper Business.

12 Little, J.W. (1990) The persistence of privacy: Autonomy and initiative in teachers' professional relations. *Teachers College Record* 91(4), pp. 509–535.

13 Hargreaves, A. (1994) *Changing teachers, changing times: Teachers' work and culture in the postmodern age*. New York: Teachers College Press, p. 186.

14 Achinstein, B. (2002) *Community, diversity, and conflict among schoolteachers: The ties that blind*. New York: Teachers College Press, p. 7.

15 Hargreaves, A., Boyle, B., & Harris, A. (2014) *Uplifting leadership: How organizations, teams, and communities raise performance*. San Francisco: Jossey-Bass.

16 See Barnett, B., Byrd, A., & Wieder, A. (2013) *Teacherpreneurs: Innovative teachers who lead but don't leave*. San Francisco: Jossey-Bass.

17 Muijs, D., Ainscow, M., Chapman, C., & West, M. (2011) *Collaboration and networking in education*. Dordrecht, Holland: Springer, p. 152.

18 Putnam, R.D. (2015) *Our kids: The American dream in crisis.* New York: Simon & Schuster.
19 Lubienski, C.A., & Lubienski, S.T. (2014) *The public school advantage: Why public schools outperform private schools.* Chicago: University of Chicago Press.
20 Lubienski & Lubienski, *The public school advantage,* p. 127.
21 Lubienski & Lubienski, *The public school advantage,* p. 133.
22 Kierkegaard, S. (2013) *Fear and trembling and the sickness unto death.* Princeton, NJ: Princeton University Press.
23 Sartre, J.-P. (1964) *Nausea.* New York: New Directions.
24 Beauvoir, S. (1948) *The ethics of ambiguity.* New York: Citadel.
25 Fromm, E. (1976) *To have or to be?* New York: Bloomsbury.
26 Maslow, A. (1966) *The psychology of science: A reconnaissance.* Chicago: Gateway.
27 May, R. (1969) *Love and will.* New York: Norton.
28 Schleiermacher, F. (2000) *Texte zur Pädagogik* [Pedagogical texts] (Vol. 2). Frankfurt: Suhrkamp, p. 13.
29 Buber, M. (1970) *I and thou.* New York: Charles Scribner's Sons.
30 Arrupe, P. (1973) *Men and women for others: Address to the Tenth International Congress of Jesuit Alumni in Europe.* Retrieved from http://onlineministries.creighton.edu/CollaborativeMinistry/men-for-others.html.
31 Hefner, R.W., & Zaman, M.Q. (Eds.) (2007) *Schooling Islam: The culture and politics of modern Muslim education.* Princeton, NJ: Princeton University Press.
32 Gowans, C.W. (2003) *Philosophy of the Buddha.* New York: Routledge.
33 Griffin, D.R. (1990) *Sacred interconnections: Postmodern spirituality, political economy, and art.* Albany: State University of New York Press.
34 Dewey, J. (1916) *Democracy and education: An introduction to the philosophy of education.* New York: Macmillan.

References

Achinstein, B. (2002) *Community, diversity, and conflict among schoolteachers: The ties that blind.* New York: Teachers College Press.
Arrupe, P. (1973) *Men and women for others: Address to the Tenth International Congress of Jesuit Alumni in Europe.* Retrieved from http://online ministries.creighton.edu/CollaborativeMinistry/men-for-others.html.
Barnett, B., Byrd, A., & Wieder, A. (2013) *Teacherpreneurs: Innovative teachers who lead but don't leave.* San Francisco: Jossey-Bass.
Beauvoir, S. (1948) *The ethics of ambiguity.* New York: Citadel.
Bryk, A.S., Gomez, L.M., Grunow, A., & LeMahieu, P.G. (2015) *Learning to improve: How America's schools can get better at getting better.* Cambridge, MA: Harvard Education Press.
Buber, M. (1970) *I and thou.* New York: Charles Scribner's Sons.
Datnow, A., & Hubbard, L. (2016) Teacher capacity for and beliefs about data-driven decision making: A literature review of international research. *Journal of Educational Change* 17(1), 7–28.
Datnow, A., & Park, V. (2014) *Data-driven leadership.* San Francisco: Jossey-Bass.
Dewey, J. (1916) *Democracy and education: An introduction to the philosophy of education.* New York: Macmillan.
Fromm, E. (1976) *To have or to be?* New York: Bloomsbury.

Gowans, C.W. (2003) *Philosophy of the Buddha*. New York: Routledge.

Griffin, D.R. (1990) *Sacred interconnections: Postmodern spirituality, political economy, and art*. Albany: State University of New York Press.

Hargreaves, A. (1994) *Changing teachers, changing times: Teachers' work and culture in the postmodern age*. New York: Teachers College Press.

Hargreaves, A., Boyle, B., & Harris, A. (2014) *Uplifting leadership: How organizations, teams, and communities raise performance*. San Francisco: Jossey-Bass.

Hattie, J. (2009) *Visible learning: A synthesis of 800 meta-analyses relating to achievement*. New York: Routledge.

Hefner, R.W., & Zaman, M.Q. (Eds.) (2007) *Schooling Islam: The culture and politics of modern Muslim education*. Princeton, NJ: Princeton University Press.

Kellerman, B. (2012) *The end of leadership*. New York: Harper Business.

Kierkegaard, S. (2013) *Fear and trembling and the sickness unto death*. Princeton, NJ: Princeton University Press.

Kirp, D.L. (2013) *Improbable scholars: The rebirth of a great American school system and a strategy for America's schools*. New York: Oxford University Press.

Little, J.W. (1990) The persistence of privacy: Autonomy and initiative in teachers' professional relations. *Teachers College Record* 91(4), 509–535.

Lubienski, C.A., & Lubienski, S.T. (2014) *The public school advantage: Why public schools outperform private schools*. Chicago: University of Chicago Press.

Maslow, A. (1966) *The psychology of science: A reconnaissance*. Chicago: Gateway.

May, R. (1969) *Love and will*. New York: Norton.

Meyer, M.A., & Meyer, H. (2007) *Wolfgang Klafki: Eine Didaktik für das 21. Jahrhundert?* [Wolfgang Klafki: A didactic for the 21st century?]. Weinheim: Beltz Verlag.

Muijs, D., Ainscow, M., Chapman, C., & West, M. (2011) *Collaboration and networking in education*. Dordrecht, Holland: Springer, p. 152.

O'Cadiz, M., Wong, P.L., & Torres, C.A. (1998) *Education and democracy: Paolo Freire, social movements, and educational reform in São Paolo*. Boulder, CO: Westview.

OECD (2014) *Measuring innovation in education: A new perspective*. Paris: OECD.

Putnam, R.D. (2015) *Our kids: The American dream in crisis*. New York: Simon & Schuster.

Saito, E., Khong, T.D.H., & Tsukui, A. (2012) Why is school reform sustained even after a project? A case study of Bac Giang Province, Vietnam. *Journal of Educational Change* 13(2), 259–287.

Sartre, J.-P. (1964) *Nausea*. New York: New Directions.

Schleiermacher, F. (2000) *Texte zur Pädagogik* [Pedagogical texts] (Vol. 2). Frankfurt: Suhrkamp.

Yessup, A. (2013) Making sure every person matters. In: Crossley, D. (Ed.) *Sustainable school transformation: An inside-out school led approach*. London: Bloomsbury, pp. 253–276.

Acknowledgments

I am grateful to many educators, scholars, and funders for their support that enabled me to study the schools, organizations, and networks that are described in this book. First and foremost, I thank the Lynch School of Education at Boston College, which has provided me with an outstanding intellectual home for the ideas in this book to develop. Andy Hargreaves provided me with indispensable ideas and support while writing this book, and I will always cherish the memories of our discussions during our hikes on the Appalachian Trail. I would like to thank Stephani Burton, Chris Bacon, Juan Cristóbal Garcia-Huidobro, Andrew Miller, Anna Nobles, Michael O'Connor, Kate Soules, and Shanee Wangia for their careful readings and advice on the text.

The German Academic Exchange Services program and the Federal Chancellor's Leadership program of the Alexander von Humboldt Foundation have supported my research in many ways for many years. I would also like to thank the Freudenberg Foundation and the Robert Bosch Foundation for their kind support.

In 2014, I was honored to receive the C.J. Koh Chair of the National Institute of Education in Singapore to present my reflections on global imperatives in educational change. I extend my profound gratitude to all of my colleagues in Singapore. Your hospitality and collegiality taught me volumes about what it means to truly recognize the role of education in social progress.

For my colleagues J.-C. Couture, Jean Stiles, and Phil McRae at the Alberta Teachers' Association and throughout the province of Alberta, I would like to express my gratitude for your unshakeable friendships and stimulating intellectual exchanges over many years.

The Critical Friends group of Education International in Brussels provided a fruitful forum for deliberation about educational change. I especially thank Fred van Leeuwen, David Edwards, Susan Hopwood, and John Bangs. Thank you as well to Beatriz Pont and Michael Schratz for your careful and conscientious readings of the manuscript while it was still in draft form.

The Rockefeller Study and Conference Center in Bellagio, Italy provided me with a residency that allowed me to develop new ideas that are expressed in this book. Thank you for this spectacular opportunity to step back and regain a big picture perspective on educational change.

Finally, I wish to thank Shelley Cochran, who has stood by me through thick and thin for over three fulfilling decades. We first met as young teachers in 1981 and her professionalism and integrity have always been a source of great inspiration to me. To see how children come alive when she is teaching and how parents express their gratitude for her dedication is to bear personal witness to the grandeur of education.

Sections of this book have previously appeared in "Three Forms of Professional Capital: Systemic, social movement, and activist" in the *Journal of Professional Capital and Community* 1(4), October 2016.

Index

Page numbers in *italics* denote tables, those in **bold** denote figures.